THE ROCK & ROLL A LEVEL

www.penguin.co.uk

THE ROCK & ROLL
A LEVEL
A VERY HARD
POP QUIZ

David Hepworth

BANTAM PRESS

TRANSWORLD PUBLISHERS
Penguin Random House, One Embassy Gardens,
8 Viaduct Gardens, London SW11 7BW
www.penguin.co.uk

Transworld is part of the Penguin Random House group of companies
whose addresses can be found at global.penguinrandomhouse.com

First published in Great Britain in 2019 by Bantam Press
an imprint of Transworld Publishers. This new edition
published by Bantam Press in 2020.

A CIP catalogue record for this book
is available from the British Library.

ISBN 9781787634398

Typeset in 11.31/13.92 pt Minion Pro by Jouve (UK), Milton Keynes
Printed and bound in Great Britain by Clays Ltd, Elcograf S.p.A.

Penguin Random House is committed to a sustainable
future for our business, our readers and our planet. This book
is made from Forest Stewardship Council® certified paper.

This book is dedicated to anyone who had an accidental education through listening to pop music.

The unteachable Debbie Harry.

INTRODUCTION

It's rarely a good idea to go looking for life lessons in the words of even the best songs, most of which will always prefer a good slogan to a fully developed thought. For instance, when in 'No Surrender' Bruce Springsteen sang, 'We learned more from a three-minute record than we ever learned in school,' he wasn't intending his words to be taken literally but he was expecting to be taken seriously.

Even Springsteen, who by his own admission spent the bulk of his schooldays staring through the classroom window and daydreaming of being a member of the Animals, clearly picked up something about how to read, write, and perform basic arithmetical calculations while attending high school in Freehold, New Jersey.

However, as soon as he could escape full-time education, that's exactly what he did. This is something he had in common with Bob Dylan, John Lennon, Paul McCartney, Mick Jagger, Keith Richards, Ray Davies, Brian Wilson, Jimi Hendrix, David Bowie, Rod Stewart, Joni Mitchell, Kate Bush and many other no-marks who were clearly never going to amount to anything, if the dire warnings of their teachers were to be believed.

These people didn't leave school because they would not have been bright enough to benefit from being educated to A level or degree level, but because they were intent on pursuing a musical career and at the time there was only one way to do this, and that was by hitting the road. In fact Bob Dylan in his high school yearbook announced his ambition was 'to join Little Richard'.

This kind of move had consequences for them as people,

which only became clearer when they got beyond thirty. They missed out on the student experience, which is such a formative stage for so many of us. At the stage of life when most of their future fans were lying in bed until midday, polishing their arguments about Marx (obviously without going to the trouble of actually reading him) and trying to get through an entire year of college without handing in so much as a single essay, these people were out there playing in front of any audience that would tolerate them, excising the last ounce of any self-consciousness they might have about demanding payment and learning lessons about human nature that their student contemporaries would take long years to learn.

That didn't mean the people who had gone off to be rock stars had no interest in the courses taught at school or college. Indeed many of them would in time make up for what they missed. They tried to educate themselves in subjects they had barely scratched the surface of when they were behind a desk. What's more, they tended to show off about it too.

The generation of rock stars who undertook the journey from rhyming 'moon' with 'June' to trying to accommodate the names of philosophers or scientists within the often rudimentary rhyme schemes of pop songs were also a great generation of autodidacts.

They taught themselves for three reasons: the first is they had the standard college dropout's remorse that they might have missed something; the second is that they realized that developing even a superficial interest in the battles of the American Civil War, the development of the geodesic dome or the Zoot Suit Riots of 1943 might give them something to talk about in interviews; the third and most important is that they realized that reading widely if unscientifically could provide them with the raw material for songs. There is nobody more inclined to pick up reading matter than the musician in the studio stuck for an idea for a song. John Lennon took the line about the number of holes in Blackburn, Lancashire from a copy of the *Daily Mail* he happened to be browsing as he composed 'A Day In The Life'.

Nobody frowns on such magpie techniques in the world of pop. It's regarded as the sign of a lively mind. And here's where the much-derided music business has always been able to hold its head up in the company of book publishers and the people who run television stations or film studios.

If a moderately successful novelist decided that her next book should diverge so markedly from its predecessor that her readers might well be perplexed, her publishers would stop her from publishing it.

If a TV actor who made his name in one kind of role suddenly wished to play its diametric opposite, his agent would sit him down and give him the hard word.

If a commercial film-maker suddenly decided his next film should be all about snow, he wouldn't even get through his elevator pitch before being booted out of the mogul's office.

It is not so in the world of music. In the world of music it is accepted that songwriters will go wherever the muse takes them and that their wanderings will often take them to some unlikely places. Kate Bush, in fact, did make an album all about snow. Stevie Wonder made one about plants. The Kinks made one about the decline and fall of the British Empire. Here's the thing. Nobody stopped them.

These artists broadened their hinterlands simply because they could. Paul McCartney, who is often regarded as one of the more conservative of his generation, began his songwriting life with 'she was just seventeen, you know what I mean'; a few years later he was writing a song about Picasso's last words.

Bruce Springsteen started out writing love songs to Sandy on the Asbury Park rollercoaster and wound up documenting the struggles of migrant workers in northern California in the manner of a latter-day John Steinbeck.

Kate Bush began by warbling about Heathcliff and eventually wrote a song about the mathematical formula known as π.

The good news is we have all been the unwitting beneficiaries of the sometimes showy precocity of the people who left school the moment they could. As a consequence of it our devotion to popular music has put us in the way of a great deal of what we might call accidental education. We probably learned the geography and the political history of the United States while listening to Chuck Berry or Bob Dylan. We all picked up a smattering of knowledge about the avant-garde from that inveterate magpie David Bowie. What little we know about the slave trade is as likely to have been gleaned from the first few albums by Bob Marley as from a history lesson on William Wilberforce. This is one of the things I have always loved about pop music.

Everybody who writes about pop music brings to it their own prejudices and proclivities. For some it's a way of writing about politics by different means. For others it's a way of writing about things that truly fascinate them, which could be glamour or money or careers or politics or even alternative forms of tuning.

I've always been fascinated by the things that pop music brought me into contact with. The book that you hold in your hand is dedicated to the proposition that the things pop music touches on are every bit as interesting as the music itself.

If you're looking for more examples of that most debased currency 'rock trivia', look elsewhere. This book couldn't be further from that. This book is rooted in my personal belief that the people who can tell you the chart positions achieved by certain records or the fact that for this track the bassist played the piano and the pianist played the flute are not the kind of people whose company you would naturally seek. That's because they are bores. It's perfectly possible to be every bit as boring on the subject of the Smiths as on the subject of underfloor heating.

On the other hand someone who knows that on the covers of three consecutive albums released in the late sixties Bob Dylan is wearing the same suede jacket, that a striking number of people who made their names in music were hospitalized as children, or that the caves of Altamira that Steely Dan sang about are the site of paintings which were begun thirty-six thousand years ago, is generally the kind of person who understands that your role in conversation is to keep up the flow and not bring it to a sudden halt.

There are two things you can do with pop music. One is simply to enjoy listening to it. The other is to enjoy its larger-than-life characters and the fantastic parallel universe that it provides. This is a world where we can watch people living a life that is in many respects just like ours and in other respects not like any life that anyone we know has ever led. The old saying 'most people in the music business are either poorer than you'd think or richer than you could possibly imagine' perfectly captures the essence of what makes it fascinating.

Some people have a tendency to say that anything that isn't all about 'the work' must necessarily fall into the category of trivia and as such ought to be beneath our dignity. From time to time somebody will even praise my writing for being 'above trivia'. This only leads me to believe they haven't read much of it. I love trivia – or, as I prefer to call it, detail. It's the details of people's lives that give them away. It's the details that provide a vital corrective to the gusts and gales of rhetoric that rock stars habitually give off in interviews. Sadly there are minds so intoxicated by this apparently elevated discourse that they cannot appreciate the joy which can always be derived from a knowledge of small things.

In the course of a life and career that has been too much occupied with talking about and listening to popular music, I have never got over my fascination with the fact that correction fluid was invented by the mother of Mike Nesmith of the Monkees; that Bruce Springsteen's daughter Jessica competes in elite show-jumping events alongside the daughters of Christina Onassis and Roman Abramovich; that working-class hero John Lennon was brought up by a woman who was the embodiment of middle-class gentility; that Bob Dylan has a habit of turning up unannounced at the childhood homes of legendary rock stars; and that Buddy Holly took that final fatal plane ride because he wanted to do his laundry before the next show.

All those small facts betray as much about the life and work of the stars involved as anything they may have cared to tell you themselves. However, I don't need that to justify the fact that I simply find such details fascinating.

This book takes its name from a competition I used to run in the 1990s when I was presenting a weekly show on the BBC's radio station in London. The idea of the competition was that it was most likely to be mastered by people who knew a certain amount about music but even more about the world beyond music and were adept at putting the two together to solve puzzles. This book, as you have doubtless noticed, is organized along the lines of a number of short exam papers in different subjects, spread across three terms with a trip between each one and at the end. We've organized it in such a way that you can test yourself on the questions and then turn the page to see the answers and see how you did. The majority of these answers are longer than would be the case in most quiz books because, well, the truth is often slightly complicated, which is what makes it interesting. It's my hope that the way in which it is organized will disadvantage the standard rock bore while giving a head start to anyone who takes a wide-ranging interest in the world. If you happen to be a rock bore, then why not invite along some significant other to play with you? You may be surprised at what the two of you can achieve together.

Finally, in an ideal world the answer to a question in a trivia quiz should be slightly more interesting than the question. That rather depends on the reader being the kind of person who is always keen to know more rather than the kind of person who feels that they know quite enough already. There's a small test here you can try on yourself. If you don't know the answer, you should, on being apprised of it, make a noise indicative of interest piqued. Something like 'ah'. If your natural inclination is to say 'So?' then I'm afraid there is very little I can do for you.

David Hepworth

CONTENTS

Self-improvement the Bill Haley way.

The Subjects

AMERICAN STUDIES

Bruce Springsteen:
made in America.

QUESTIONS

Post-war popular music was forged as a result of the transatlantic traffic in ideas and styles between two nations of English-speaking people; or 'two nations divided by a common language', as George Bernard Shaw, an Irishman, described them. This opening section explores our fascination with a place we only think we understand.

1 In 1965, David Jones changed his name to David Bowie in honour of the famous American frontiersman Jim Bowie who died at which famous battle?

2 What American city do the following songs have in common: 'By The Time I Get To Phoenix' by Jimmy Webb, 'Promised Land' by Chuck Berry and 'The King Of Rock'n'Roll' by Prefab Sprout's Paddy McAloon?

3 In the years before the Beatles came along just three British acts had enjoyed number one hits in the *Billboard* charts. They all happened in the same year. They were all instrumentals. Two of the records were also UK number ones. The third was made by a band leader who was born in London and then emigrated to the United States. Can you name all three?

4 Did Elvis Presley ever perform live outside the continental United States?

5 The theme tune to ITV's current affairs show of the seventies and eighties *Weekend World* was Mountain's 'Nantucket Sleighride'. What is a Nantucket sleighride?

6 US banknotes are often referred to in hip hop as Dead Presidents because of the people whose faces are often shown on them. The current series, issued from 2003, features Abraham Lincoln, Alexander Hamilton, Andrew Jackson, Ulysses S. Grant and Benjamin Franklin. Which two of those five are not Dead Presidents?

7 What record, which got to number two in the UK singles chart in 1981, has among its lyrics a series of words closely associated with the United States Postal Service?

8 Drake, Arcade Fire, Neil Young and Nelly Furtado are all huge stars in America. Where do they come from?

9 Did John Lennon ever become a US citizen?

10 What's the link between *Coronation Street* and the Beatles' first appearance on *The Ed Sullivan Show* in 1964?

ANSWERS

1 The Battle of the Alamo.

It was violence that made Jim Bowie famous. He killed a sheriff with a long knife that henceforth bore his name. Bowie was one of the two hundred defenders of the Alamo who were killed when the Mexican army took the old mission on 6 March 1836.

2 Albuquerque.

The city that all three songs have in common is the largest in New Mexico. It's one of the cities the fleeing protagonist passes through in Jimmy Webb's 'By The Time I Get To Phoenix', Chuck Berry's hero wakes up high over Albuquerque in 'Promised Land', and the chorus of Prefab Sprout's 'King Of Rock'n'Roll' simply goes 'hot dog, jumping frog, Albuquerque'.

3 Acker Bilk's 'Stranger On The Shore', the Tornados' 'Telstar' and 'The Stripper' by David Rose.

Rose had been born in London but moved to Chicago as a child. All three songs went to the top of the US chart in 1962. The Beatles had six number one singles in the US chart in 1964 alone.

4 Yes – twice.

Elvis Presley performed live on just two occasions outside the continental United States: he visited Canada in 1957, and in 1973 he played a concert in Hawaii that was broadcast worldwide by satellite. Hawaii is the fiftieth state of the union but it is outside the North American continent.

5 It's a whaling term.

A Nantucket sleighride is a reference to the days when the bloody business of whaling was conducted from open boats. When the harpoon pierced the whale the creature would set off, pulling the boat and its occupants with it in a grisly slalom that took its name from the Massachusetts port where the whaling industry was based.

6 Alexander Hamilton and Benjamin Franklin.

These were the two founding fathers of the United States who got their pictures on the currency despite never being President. Hamilton established the new nation's financial system and over two hundred years later had the honour of a hit musical based on his life. Benjamin Franklin was never President, being too busy discovering electricity and inventing bifocal spectacles.

7 'O Superman' by Laurie Anderson.

Part of the lyrics of this 1981 hit go 'Neither snow nor rain nor gloom of night shall stay these couriers from the swift completion of their appointed rounds'.

The translation from Herodotus is not strictly the motto of the US Postal Service but it's inscribed across the top of the main New York Post Office facing Penn Station and is closely associated with the historic role of what remains one of the few national organizations in the USA.

8 They all come from Canada.

9 No.

John Lennon left Britain in 1971 and never came back. He was given his green card, allowing him to be a Resident Alien, in 1976 and was later informed that he would be eligible for citizenship in 1981. He was murdered at the end of 1980.

10 Davy Jones.

The epoch-making edition of *The Ed Sullivan Show* of 9 February 1964, when an estimated seventy-five million Americans got their first glimpse of the Beatles, had been designed as an all-British affair. Elsewhere on the bill were Tessie O'Shea, Britain's answer to Sophie Tucker, and British members of the Broadway cast of Lionel Bart's *Oliver!*, among them a young actor called Davy Jones. Jones would become a scream idol himself within a couple of years as a member of the Monkees. At the time his major claim to fame was having appeared on ITV's hit soap *Coronation Street* in the role of Ena Sharples' nephew.

'If I'd lived in Roman times, I'd have lived in Rome. Today, America is the Roman Empire and now New York is Rome itself.'

John Lennon

ART

Joni Mitchell and Ronnie Wood, handy with a brush.

QUESTIONS

Many's the album cover that has appropriated fine art whole-sale. Examples of this range from Jeff Beck's swiping of René Magritte's giant apple for the cover of his 1969 album Beck-Ola *to Peter Saville's borrowing of a photograph of the Appiani family tomb for Joy Division's* Closer. *More interesting are the cases where acts have borrowed a well-known image and given it their own individual tweak. We do not encourage the use of Google in coming up with answers to a round in this quiz. However, this is one case where you could do an image search without spoiling your own fun. Each of these famous paintings has been borrowed or pastiched for the cover of a rock album. What are the albums?*

1 *The Snake Charmer* by Henri Rousseau
2 *School of Athens* by Raphael
3 *The Raft of the Medusa* by Théodore Géricault
4 *Bal du moulin de la Galette* by Auguste Renoir
5 *The Empire of Light* by René Magritte
6 *The Swing* by Jean-Honoré Fragonard
7 *Self-Portrait with Bandaged Ear* by Vincent van Gogh
8 *Le Déjeuner sur l'herbe* by Édouard Manet
9 *The Last Supper* by Leonardo da Vinci
10 *Bacchus and Ariadne* by Titian

ANSWERS

1 *Tango In The Night.*

Henri 'Le Douanier' Rousseau painted *The Snake Charmer* in Paris in 1907. Like many of his paintings it depicted a lush, exotic jungle such as he had never actually visited. (Rousseau got all the inspiration he needed by visiting the botanical garden.) In the 1980s Australian artist Brett-Livingstone Strong, who had carved out a nice career making statues of the likes of Michael Jackson and John Lennon, produced a painting called *Homage a Henri Rousseau*, which was bought by Lindsey Buckingham and became the cover of Fleetwood Mac's 1987 album.

2 *Use Your Illusion.*

Raphael's fresco *School of Athens* was originally commissioned for the Vatican in 1510. A detail from its vast depiction of Greek philosophers hard at their brow-wrinkling trade was pinched by Guns N' Roses for their 1991 release, and adapted by artist Mark Kostabi. It was then chosen by Axl Rose as the ideal image for the cover of both volumes of their much-anticipated album.

3 *Rum, Sodomy & The Lash.*

Géricault's *The Raft of the Medusa* is pastiched by the Pogues on *Rum, Sodomy & The Lash* with members of the band replacing those clinging to the raft. The album gets its title from Churchill's acid answer when asked to list the traditions of the Royal Navy. Churchill was never more an army man than in this instance.

4 *A Night On The Town.*

Renoir's *Bal du moulin de la Galette* is pastiched on the cover of this 1976 album by Rod Stewart with the boy himself placed among the Parisian revellers.

5 *Late For The Sky.*

Magritte's *Empire of Light*, which plays with the idea of a night-time street scene set against a daytime sky, was the inspiration behind the design of Jackson Browne's 1974 album. The credits say 'cover concept Jackson Browne if it's all reet with Magritte'.

6 *Sailin' Shoes.*

In *The Swing* by the eighteenth-century French painter Fragonard, a beautiful woman amuses herself on a swing while a gentleman admires her unseen. In Neon Park's adaptation of the idea for the cover of the 1972 Little Feat album, the lady is replaced by a cake and the admirer by a snail. In a further nod to classical painting her swing has been launched by Gainsborough's 'Blue Boy'.

7 *Turbulent Indigo.*

The title track of Joni Mitchell's 1994 album refers to Van Gogh. Hence she painted herself for the cover after the style of the artist's *Self-Portrait with Bandaged Ear.* At the time she felt her work was being rejected while lesser artists were being embraced and she identified with the artist who reputedly never sold any paintings. 'So, rather than physically cut my ear off, I did it in effigy.'

8 *See Jungle! See Jungle! Go Join Your Gang Yeah, City All Over! Go Ape Crazy!*

Manet's 1863 painting *Le Déjeuner sur l'herbe* was pastiched by Bow Wow Wow for the cover of this 1981 album. The original painting caused a scandal in Paris for showing a naked woman enjoying a picnic alongside two fully dressed men. The photographic tribute was shot by Andy Earl in a wood near Priory Park in Surrey. The group's singer Annabella Lwin didn't know she would be required to take her clothes off until her manager Malcolm McLaren told her when she turned up. Nor did the photographer know she was only fourteen at the time. The same painting was also pastiched on the cover of Lowell George's solo album *Thanks I'll Eat It Here.*

9 *Gang Signs & Prayer.*

This 2017 album by Stormzy echoes the construction of Leonardo da Vinci's late fifteenth-century depiction of the Last Supper with the artist in the position of Christ and his friends, all wearing black balaclavas, surrounding him, with a small child in the position of Judas Iscariot.

10 *God Shuffled His Feet.*

For their biggest album, in 1993, the Canadian band Crash Test Dummies had their faces superimposed on the naked figures of the characters in Titian's 1522 painting *Bacchus and Ariadne*.

BIOLOGY

Ian Anderson of Jethro Tull in his remarkable hose.

QUESTIONS

Richard Dawkins says that while physics is the study of the simpler things in the universe, biology is the study of the complex things. Since its raw material is life itself it's not surprising that pop music has not always stuck strictly to the facts when it comes to borrowing bits and pieces of biology. Here are ten places where pop music has at least tried.

1 Biology is the study of life in all its forms. Many pop groups have attempted to sum up in song what exactly life is. What conclusions about life did the following come to in the titles of their songs?

    a) 10cc
    b) Talk Talk
    c) Jethro Tull
    d) Ronan Keating

2 Speaking of the life force, what is the name of the instrumental hit from the year 1973 that was originally on an album called *They Only Come Out At Night* and was named after an 1818 novel by Mary Shelley which was subtitled 'The Modern Prometheus'?

3 Biology encompasses the study of many different creatures, which brings us to the name of the last resident dance troupe on *Top of the Pops*, an ensemble that followed in the footsteps of the Go-Jos, Pan's People, Ruby Flipper and Legs & Co. What was this twenty-strong group called?

4 Which 1979 double album was inspired by a best-selling book of pseudoscience, a book which claimed that human beings and plants could communicate?

5 It's often said that pop protest songs rarely actually achieve anything. However, there is one thing that Joni Mitchell sang about in 'Big Yellow Taxi' that did actually come to pass. What is it?

6 What's the molecule carrying all our genetic code that has inspired songs by Little Mix, Kendrick Lamar and A Flock of Seagulls?

7 The animal kingdom breaks down into six categories: invertebrates, mammals, birds, amphibians, reptiles and fish. Put these bands, which are all named – in some cases punningly – after animals, into their appropriate categories.

    a) the Black Crowes
    b) the Beatles
    c) the Flying Lizards
    d) Box of Frogs
    e) Eels
    f) White Whale

8 Which theoretically planet-saving song was Michael Jackson singing at the 1996 Brit Awards when Jarvis Cocker felt moved to take to the stage and show his disrespect?

9 What are the biological terms that supplied the titles for albums by Franz Ferdinand, the Human League and Todd Rundgren?

10 Which animal-loving musician wrote a song that announced he had had enough of landlubber women and was minded to grow fins and take up with a mermaid?

ANSWERS

1
a) 'Life Is A Minestrone'
b) 'Life's What You Make It'
c) 'Life's A Long Song'
d) 'Life Is A Rollercoaster'

2 'Frankenstein' by the Edgar Winter Group.

3 Zoo.

They began in 1981 and finished two years later.

4 Stevie Wonder's *Journey Through The Secret Life Of Plants*.

It was based on the book *The Secret Life of Plants* by Peter Tompkins and Christopher Bird which came out in 1973. Wonder composed his album by having each sequence in the subsequent film described to him and then supplying music for it. It is fair to say it was not well received.

5 The DDT ban.

In 'Big Yellow Taxi', Mitchell begs the farmer to 'put away the DDT'. In 1972, just two years after the song came out, the use of the insecticide was banned in the United States and since then there has been a worldwide ban on its use except in very special circumstances.

6 DNA.

Little Mix and Kendrick Lamar have both had success with songs with that title in recent years, while the Flock of Seagulls instrumental of that name won a Grammy in 1983.

7
a) the Black Crowes are birds
b) the Beatles, at least in their original spelling, are invertebrates
c) the Flying Lizards are reptiles
d) Box of Frogs are amphibians
e) Eels belong to the fish family
f) White Whale are mammals

8 'Earth Song'.

The song Jackson was singing, his own 'Earth Song', climaxed with the Pepsi pitchman singing 'What about the common man?' from the top of a hydraulic tower that had hauled him above a crowd of extras who looked beseechingly in his direction as though he was the greatest truth teller to come down the pike since Jesus Christ preached his sermon on the mount. Cocker couldn't resist the opportunity to climb on to the stage amid the resulting confusion and indicate his displeasure by waggling his backside in Jackson's direction.

9 *Blood*, which was the name of a 2009 album by Franz Ferdinand, carries oxygen to and carbon dioxide from the tissues of our bodies. *Reproduction*, the title of a Human League album released in 1979, is the biological process by which new organisms are produced by parents. *Runt*, the title of a 1970 Todd Rundgren record, is the term for the smallest and weakest of a litter in the animal world.

10 Captain Beefheart, who made just such a promise on 'Grow Fins' from his 1972 album *The Spotlight Kid*.

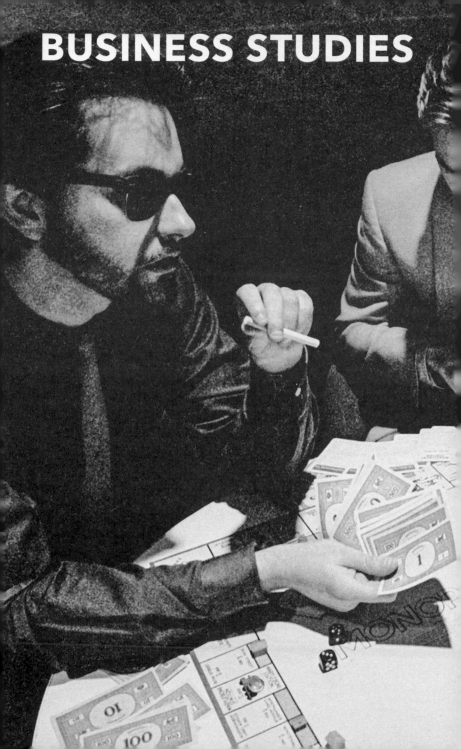

BUSINESS STUDIES

Board of Heaven 17 discuss cash flow.

QUESTIONS

Pop music is a form of commercial art. Omit the commerce and you are failing to properly understand the art. Nobody in pop music ever did anything out of pure motives. Almost every move has its fiduciary component. This is of course what makes it interesting. This round deals with managers and money, two things rarely far from the thoughts of even the most elevated sort of performer.

1 What's the simple explanation for why Elvis Presley never toured overseas?

2 Which rap star went from a net worth of $30 million to bankruptcy in just six years, thanks in small part to building a house that had garaging for his seventeen cars?

3 Which performer was reputed to have been paid $15 million for just one season as a judge on the TV programme *The X Factor*?

4 Larry Parnes, the most famous British manager of rock & roll stars of the late fifties and early sixties, was fond of giving his charges new names that supposedly went with what he imagined to be their erotic potential. How many of his clients can you name?

5 Which record companies had the following slogans?

a) 'The greatest recording organization in the world'

b) 'The sound of Young America'

c) 'If they're dead, we'll sign 'em'

6 Where did Albert Grossman, who was Bob Dylan's manager, die in 1986?

7 Who was part-credited with the composition of Chuck Berry's multimillion-selling hit 'Maybellene' despite having absolutely nothing to do with the song at all?

8 How much did *Saturday Night Live* producer Lorne Michaels offer the Beatles if they would reunite and perform three songs on the long-running comedy show in 1976?

9 Which group arranged for their entire £8,000 fee to cascade down upon the audience at the end of a gig at the Hammersmith Odeon in 1976?

10 Who came out of retirement in his seventies in order to earn back the money his business manager had embezzled from him?

ANSWERS

1 Because his manager had no passport.

Elvis never toured overseas because Colonel Tom Parker was born Andreas Cornelis van Kuijk in Holland in 1909, entered the United States illegally in 1926 and never held a US passport. When Elvis was in the army in Europe between 1958 and 1960 Parker never visited him, despite spending most of the time worried that other managers would try to tempt his golden boy away.

2 MC Hammer.

Stanley Kirk Burrell, better known as MC Hammer, was a huge-selling artist in the late eighties and he used his wealth to put all his extended family on the payroll and to build his own personal Xanadu overlooking the poor area where he had come from. By 1996 he had filed for Chapter 11 bankruptcy. His career trajectory is the perfect illustration of the old music saw that stars are either poorer than you would think or richer than you could possibly imagine. Some of them manage to be both.

3 Britney Spears.

In an attempt to establish the British hit TV show with American audiences and to overhaul market leader *The Voice*, Simon Cowell signed Spears to be a judge on the second season of Fox Television's *The X Factor* in 2012. He initially offered $10 million and was bid up to $15 million. The arrangement lasted for just one season as the programme failed to dislodge the competition.

4 You could have had Tommy Steele, Billy Fury, Marty Wilde, Vince Eager, Duffy Power, Johnny Gentle, Dickie Pride, Lance Fortune, Georgie Fame and even the less well-known Nelson Keene. It is said that Joe Brown stuck with his original name after resisting Parnes' plans to launch him as Elmer Twitch.

5 EMI Records called itself 'the greatest recording organization in the world', Motown was proud to provide 'the sound of Young America', while the independent label Stiff, which also boasted it was 'surfing on the new wave', used the slogan 'if they're dead, we'll sign 'em'.

6 On Concorde.

Albert Grossman suffered a fatal heart attack on the supersonic jet during a flight from New York to London.

7 Alan Freed.

The American DJ did an enormous amount to popularize rock music in the 1950s. Chess Records put pressure on Berry to give him 25 per cent of the credit, and therefore a quarter of the revenue, in exchange for his playing 'Maybellene' on the radio.

8 $3,000.

This generous sum was the show's standard performance fee for a four-piece band at the time. Michaels had the cheque drawn up and showed it on the air. 'You can split it any way you want to. If you want to give Ringo less that's entirely up to you.' What Michaels didn't know was that on that very night McCartney and Lennon were watching the show live in Lennon's Dakota apartment and briefly considered going down to the studio and claiming the fee.

9 Steeleye Span.

The British folk group were at the time managed by Tony Secunda, who had always been fond of a publicity stunt. It took the audience on the night some time to realize what was going on, and even longer to actually grasp the floating notes.

10 Leonard Cohen.

The singer-songwriter-poet had effectively retired when, in 2004, he discovered that Kelley Lynch, his business manager, had stolen much of the money he had set aside for his old age. To try to make up the deficit he went back on the road in 2008 and carried on touring, in front of audiences who were more numerous than ever before and who also paid more money for a ticket, until 2013. He died in 2016.

'When things get really bad, just raise your glass and stamp your feet and do a little jig. That's about all you can do.'

Leonard Cohen

CLASSICS

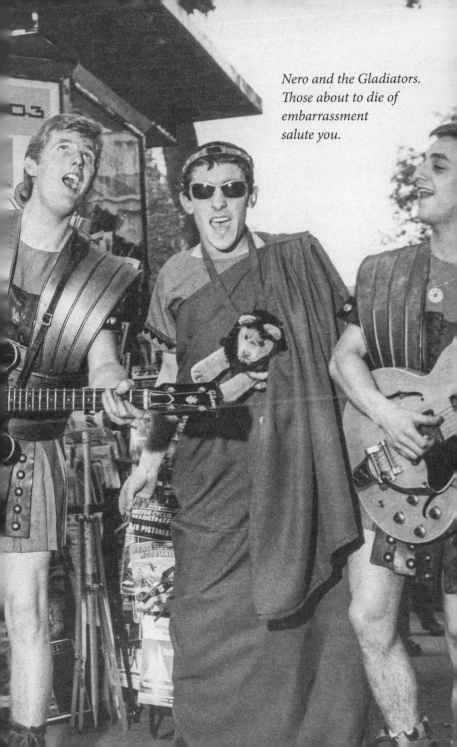

Nero and the Gladiators.
Those about to die of
embarrassment
salute you.

QUESTIONS

The ancient world of Rome and Greece, of Troy and Carthage and Egypt, still shows through in the most unexpected ways in our culture several thousand years later. The annals of antiquity are regularly ransacked for rock inspiration and references can resurface in the least-expected quarters. Here are ten examples.

1 Name the pop star, who made the top-selling album of 2001, who shares a first name with the first Queen of Carthage.

2 The lyrics of the sole big hit by a duo from Boston who went on to develop a successful sideline in children's music referred to the gang who went looking for the Golden Fleece. Who were the duo?

3 What's the name of the psych rock masterpiece from 1967 which celebrates the fearless exploits of the King of Ithaca?

4 What's the name of the hit progressive rock album from 1970 which was named after the Greek god of the sea?

5 What's the eternally appealing British group whose name is Latin for 'beyond these things'?

6 The ancient Roman goddess of love has inspired more than one pop songwriter, including Lady Gaga and Television's Tom Verlaine. What was her name?

7 Which band from the East End of London mined the ancient world for tracks like 'Alexander The Great' and 'Flight Of Icarus'?

8 Pink Floyd recorded a piece of music named after a king of Corinth, a figure in Greek mythology who was condemned to spend eternity pushing a boulder up a mountain only to see it roll down again. What was the name of the piece of music, and what album was it on?

9 Which British beat group of the early 1960s performed in tunics and togas?

10 Which all-girl trio from Birmingham named themselves after the last ruler of the Ptolemaic kingdom of Egypt?

ANSWERS

1 Dido.

Carthage, which was a major power in the first millennium BC, was situated in north-west Africa, and had a queen named Dido. Dido Florian Cloud de Bounevialle O'Malley Armstrong's first album *No Angel* sold twenty-one million copies worldwide in 2001, which is a quantity from a world no less vanished than Carthage.

2 They Might Be Giants.

In their hit 'Birdhouse In Your Soul' the singer recalls an ancestor of his whose job was to kill off Jason 'and countless screaming Argonauts'.

3 'Tales Of Brave Ulysses'.

This song celebrating the deeds of the king who was known to the Greeks as Odysseus, from the 1967 Cream album *Disraeli Gears*, was written by Eric Clapton and Martin Sharp. The latter was Clapton's flatmate at the time and provided the illustration on the cover of the LP.

4 *In The Wake Of Poseidon* by King Crimson.

5 Procol Harum.

6 Venus.

7 Iron Maiden.

8 'Sysyphus'.

The track, an instrumental by Richard Wright, was on the 1969 album *Ummagumma*.

9 Nero and the Gladiators.

Former members of this largely instrumental group included Diz Disley and Foreigner's Mick Jones.

10 Cleopatra.

This all-girl trio, whose lead singer Cleopatra Higgins was named after the legendary queen, had a number of hits in the UK at the end of the twentieth century.

ECONOMICS

Holly Johnson and flat-pack President.

QUESTIONS

Money, either the lack of it or particularly imaginative ways of spending it, is never far away from the thoughts of people in the popular music game. This round focuses on the play between music and powerful economic forces. It's where pop intersects with finance. Which it always does.

1 What was the big hit record that included the word 'Reaganomics'?

2 Who are the two British political leaders mentioned by name in George Harrison's song 'Taxman' on the album *Revolver*?

3 Who is the only political economist represented on the cover of the Beatles' *Sgt. Pepper's Lonely Hearts Club Band*?

4 Steely Dan wrote a song about the events of 24 September 1869. What is the name of the song, and what exactly happened that day?

5 Many songwriters have written songs about money in order to make points about life. What conclusions were reached about the significance of money by the following artists?

a) Cyndi Lauper
b) the Notorious B.I.G.
c) Puff Daddy
d) Wu-Tang Clan

6 What's the song by the Jam which encourages its hero to enjoy the opportunities that have opened up for him now that he's been made redundant?

7 All record deals begin with champagne and starry eyes and end in bitterness, and in some cases a song expressing the artist's bitterness towards the hand that formerly fed them. Name the anti-record company songs done by the following:

a) Sex Pistols
b) Graham Parker
c) the Clash
d) Amanda Palmer

8 There are many songs about scarcity but only a few that celebrate surplus. Name the songs by the following that fall into this category:

a) the Weather Girls
b) the Marvelettes
c) Flight of the Conchords
d) Soulwax

9 Which song boasts that the singer has a mansion, 'forget the price'?

10 When Willie Nelson heard his house was about to be raided by the Internal Revenue Service who wished to seize property in lieu of owed tax, he asked his daughter to make sure she removed Trigger before the raid. What (or who) is 'Trigger'?

ANSWERS

1 'Money's Too Tight (To Mention)'.

Reaganomics was mentioned in this hit song which was first released by the Valentine Brothers in 1982 then covered by Simply Red three years later.

2 Mr (Harold) Wilson, who was the Labour leader in 1966 when this song was written, and his Conservative opposite number Mr (Edward) Heath.

3 Karl Marx.

The author of *Das Kapital* and *The Communist Manifesto* is between Oliver Hardy and H. G. Wells.

4 The song is 'Black Friday' from the 1975 album *Katy Lied*. The lyrics describe the financial carnage that occurred in 1869 as a result of two US speculators attempting to corner the market in gold. They were ruined when the government started selling some of its own reserves, causing the price to plunge. Walter Becker and Donald Fagen used some artistic licence, such as when they mentioned catching 'the grey men when they dive from the fourteenth floor'. America's first skyscraper was not built until 1885 and topped out at a mere ten stories.

5 a) Cyndi Lauper's 1984 hit asserted that 'Money Changes Everything'

b) 'Mo Money Mo Problems' reflected the Notorious B.I.G. in 1997

c) in 1997 Puff Daddy promoted the belief that 'It's All About The Benjamins', so called in honour of the $100 bills which feature the portrait of Benjamin Franklin

d) Wu-Tang Clan made the most sweeping statement on the subject with their 1994 record 'C.R.E.A.M.', which stands for 'cash rules everything around me'

6 'Smithers-Jones'.

It was written by Bruce Foxton for the Jam's 1979 album *Setting Sons* and describes a hapless commuter in a pinstripe suit who turns up to work only to find he's surplus to requirements. In the last verse he's lyrically advised to 'put on the kettle and make some tea . . . it's time to relax, now you've worked your arse off'.

7 a) 'E.M.I.' ('they only did it 'cause of fame'), which the Pistols put on their first album on Virgin

b) 'Mercury Poisoning', about the failure of Parker's American record label to promote him properly ('I got Mercury poisoning – the best-kept secret in the West')

c) 'Complete Control', in which the Clash aired their A&R disagreements with CBS ('they said release "Remote Control", but we didn't want it on the label')

d) best of all, 'Please Drop Me', former Dresden Dolls singer Amanda Palmer's address to her record label Roadrunner ('I'm tired of sucking corporate dick')

8
a) 'It's Raining Men'
b) 'Too Many Fish In The Sea'
c) 'Too Many Dicks (On The Dance Floor)'
d) 'Too Many DJs'

9 'Life's Been Good' by Joe Walsh.

The song's rock star protagonist has forgotten the price of his mansion.

10 Trigger was Nelson's name for his favourite guitar.

'As long as I got my guitar I'll be fine,' he said. And he was. After the instrument was rescued from his house he used it to record a special album called *The IRS Tapes* which he sold direct to fans, thereby helping to pay off his debt. When Nelson's possessions were auctioned off by the IRS they were bought by fans who then gave them back to Nelson.

ENGLISH LANGUAGE

Beastie Boys park early smart car.

QUESTIONS

The name Elvis was unknown to most people until Elvis Presley became famous. The name of the most successful pop group of all time, the Beatles, looked strange to everyone when they first came along. The first word in the name Led Zeppelin was deliberately misspelled to stop people mispronouncing it. The annals of popular music are littered with proper names that people are inclined to get wrong because they try to make them look right. These are the ones that always set off the sirens on the desks occupied by subeditors on music magazines. Can you correctly spell and punctuate the names of the following acts and records?

1 The first one is the name of the duo formed by an ex-member of Bananarama and the composer of Eric Clapton's 'Lay Down Sally', who together went to number one in the UK in 1992 with 'Stay'.

2 These albums by Nick Drake, Fairport Convention and Genesis followed the brief fashion in the late sixties and early seventies for LPs with archaically spelled names.

3 The Canadian singer whose album *Ingénue* was an international hit is a unique case in music but there are precedents in the world of poetry.

4 One of the most commonly misspelled names in popular music is the surname of the former leader of the Commodores who was famous in his own right for 'Dancing On The Ceiling' and 'Hello'.

5 This three-piece metal band from Northern Ireland whose album *Troublegum* was nominated for the Mercury Music Prize in 1994 has a standard name with an unusual twist at the end.

These next five song titles all contain brackets – but where do the brackets go?

6 'You Gotta Fight For Your Right To Party!' by the Beastie Boys.

7 'Sittin' On The Dock Of The Bay' by Otis Redding.

8 'Norwegian Wood This Bird Has Flown' by the Beatles.

9 'I Can't Get No Satisfaction' by the Rolling Stones.

10 'You Make Me Feel Like A Natural Woman' by Aretha Franklin.

ANSWERS

1 The group formed by Siobhan Fahey and Marcella Detroit (formerly Marcy Levy when she was in Clapton's band) was known as Shakespears Sister. 'Shakespeare's Sister', with the 'e' at the end of the surname and the apostrophe after it, is a song by the Smiths. Both were omitted in an early piece of artwork for Fahey and Detroit's act so they decided to keep it that way.

2 *Bryter Layter* (Nick Drake, 1971), *Liege & Lief* (Fairport Convention, 1969) and *Nursery Cryme* (Genesis, 1971).

3 Kathryn Dawn Lang decided to be professionally known as the lower-case k. d. lang in emulation of the poet e. e. cummings (himself also sometimes styled e e cummings).

4 Lionel Richie has the most widely misspelled name in popular music. There is not now nor was there in the past nor will there be in the future any 't' in his name. This is news that has yet to get through to most subeditors.

5 The band were initially known as Therapy until a blunder with Letraset put a question mark at the end. They couldn't be bothered to change it so they were henceforth Therapy?

6 '(You Gotta) Fight For Your Right (To Party!)'.

7 '(Sittin' On) The Dock Of The Bay'.

8 'Norwegian Wood (This Bird Has Flown)'.

9 '(I Can't Get No) Satisfaction'.

10 '(You Make Me Feel Like) A Natural Woman'.

FASHION AND DESIGN

*Rolling Stones
grooming session.*

QUESTIONS

Where pop music is concerned appearances always matter, often more than the music itself, and only incurable snobs remain unaware of the fact. And this applies just as much to the acts who give the impression of not caring as it does to those who are openly image-conscious. Appearances matter every bit as much to the 1975 as they do to Little Mix. The ten questions that follow all relate to memorable aspects of fashion, hairstyle and make-up, and range from the impeccable to the unfortunate.

1 Which artist made his first appearance on national television in 1964 as the representative of the Society for the Prevention of Cruelty to Long-haired Men?

2 The distinctive hairstyle known as the mullet, which has been sported at different times by everyone from Billy Ray Cyrus to Michael Hutchence, was given its name by which musician?

3 What do the covers of Madonna's *Like A Prayer*, Bruce Springsteen's *Born In The U.S.A.* and the Rolling Stones' *Sticky Fingers* have in common?

4 Which band copyrighted the characteristic looks of their individual members, looks they referred to as the Catman, the Spaceman, the Demon and the Starchild?

5 Which memorable pop star look was hastily improvised before the 1997 Brit Awards through the addition of a tea towel?

6 Which accessory have Dead or Alive, TLC, David Bowie, and Dr. Hook and the Medicine Show had in common at one time or another?

7 The cover of which famous seventies album credited the artist's wife with sewing the patches on his jeans?

8 On 13 October 1961 John Lennon and Paul McCartney asked Jürgen Vollmer, a German friend of theirs, to remodel their hair into the style that Vollmer was already sporting at the time. It was a style that he had based on the fashionable youth of which city?

9 Speaking of hair, who's the odd one out in this list: Debbie Harry, Elvis Presley, Sting?

10 Bob Dylan wears the same jacket on the cover of three of his best-known LPs. Which are they?

ANSWERS

1 David Bowie.

The artist who appeared on the BBC magazine show *Tonight* in 1964 was at the time called David Jones.

2 Mike D of the Beastie Boys.

The hairstyle known as the mullet, which even David Bowie succumbed to at one point, was given its name in a piece Mike D wrote for the magazine *Grand Royal* in 1995 where he talked about 'mullet-headed people'. The Beasties recorded a song entitled 'Mullet Head', which was the first time the term had been used in a tonsorial context. Before then, since the nineteenth century, the word 'mullet' had been widely used to describe people of limited intelligence.

3 Jeans.

The covers of all three albums feature the mid-section of figures wearing jeans. In the case of the Stones album more than one intimate of the sleeve's designer Andy Warhol has subsequently claimed they modelled for the picture.

4 Kiss.

All four members of Kiss each had their own copyrighted make-up design. Paul Stanley's was the

Starchild, Gene Simmons' the Demon, Ace Frehley's the Spaceman and Peter Criss's the Catman. When the latter pair left the band their looks were bequeathed to their replacements.

5 When the Spice Girls were preparing to perform at the Brit Awards in 1997 Geri Halliwell thought her plain black minidress needed livening up so she went to visit her sister who quickly customized it with the addition of a Union Jack tea towel. Coming at the height of Britpop, this look defined both the Spice Girls and the era. It was subsequently sold for over £40,000 with the proceeds going to charity.

6 An eyepatch.

For reasons of necessity or purely for show.

7 *After The Gold Rush.*

The back cover of Neil Young's 1970 album is occupied with a close-up of the artfully patched backside of the artist's jeans. Among the credits there is one that reads 'Patches: Susan Young'. Within a year Neil and Susan would no longer be together and it is said that the patches, some of which she had attached using her own hair as thread, were unpicked by Neil's new girlfriend Carrie Snodgress.

8 Paris.

The boyish, combed-forward style, which marked a break with the slicked-back hair fashions of the previous decade, was popular with the fashionable young people of the French capital, which was where the Beatles first tried their new look.

9 Elvis Presley.

The odd one out is the King because, although he was known for his apparently jet-black hair, he was in fact the only natural blond of the three. Even as a teenager Elvis still had blond hair; he first began dyeing it black in emulation of his hero Tony Curtis. Sting, like the rest of the Police, had his hair dyed blond for an appearance in a commercial for chewing gum. Debbie Harry's dye job deliberately left her roots untouched to make it clear that she was only trying to be glamorous up to a point.

10 *Blonde On Blonde*, *John Wesley Harding* and *Nashville Skyline*.

Dylan also wears the battered old suede jacket on the cover of his first *Greatest Hits*.

*The ineffably sexy
Serge Gainsbourg
and Jane Birkin.*

FRENCH

QUESTIONS

French is one of the romance languages. This is not simply because it is proven to be the best tongue in which to whisper endearments but because it is one of those languages that emerged as a result of Roman conquest. Although France is the United Kingdom's nearest neighbour, French and British pop often seem to occupy different worlds. That has not always been the case. Here are ten instances of cultural exchange across La Manche.

1 Which British album of the 1960s was given the French title *Quatre Garçons Dans Le Vent*?

2 Which album by a Welshman was named after Canadian historian Margaret MacMillan's book about the peace conference that followed the First World War?

3 Which artist, who represented Switzerland in the Eurovision Song Contest of 1988 and sang 'God Bless America' at the *America: A Tribute to Heroes* telethon in 2001, married her manager in 1994 in a ceremony that was screened live on the national TV service of a third country?

4 Which iconic French singing star adopted a name inspired by a famous English portrait and landscape painter of the eighteenth century?

5 Which French First Lady released an album of musical settings of poems by Emily Dickinson, Yeats, Auden and Dorothy Parker?

6 John Lennon smoked which brand of French cigarette in the hope, he liked to say, of making his voice deeper?

7 In the Kraftwerk song, the Trans-Europe Express leaves Paris and travels to which two other European cities?

8 The French national anthem was featured on which UK number one record from 1967?

9 She shares a surname with a former England footballer, made her name as the leader of a group, but now wishes to be known as Chris. Who is she?

10 Sylvie Vartan's hit 'L'Amour C'est Comme Une Cigarette' is based on which UK hit record?

ANSWERS

1 *A Hard Day's Night.*

The film too was known to the French public as *Quatre Garçons Dans Le Vent*. For those whose French did not get beyond the first year, this should be taken to mean 'four trendy young men' and not 'four boys in the wind'.

2 *Paris 1919.*

John Cale's third solo album, which came out in 1973, was inspired by the book *Paris 1919: Six Months That Changed the World*, whose author, Margaret MacMillan, was the great-granddaughter of David Lloyd George. Cale appears on the cover in the costume of one of the diplomats who gathered in the French capital to decide who should pay for the war that had just finished. The decisions arrived at in Paris accidentally set in train the events that led to the next conflagration.

3 Celine Dion.

The French-Canadian singer was only twelve when she met manager René Angélil; he was already thirty-eight. He believed in her talent and approved of her relentless ambition. When she decided she wanted to make it beyond Francophone Canada he sent her to school to improve her English and to the dentist to fix her teeth. She won the Eurovision Song Contest in 1988 while representing Switzerland. When she married Angélil in 1994 in Montreal it was an event of such national importance that the ceremony was broadcast live on Canadian national TV.

4 Serge Gainsbourg.

Lucien Ginsburg changed his first name to Serge in order to pay respect to his Russian forebears, and his second name to Gainsbourg to reflect his admiration for the eighteenth-century English painter Thomas Gainsborough. It was as Serge Gainsbourg that he became one of France's best-loved and most provocative musical performers.

5 Carla Bruni.

Born of Italian parents, Bruni made her name as a model and released her first album in 2002. Her second album, 2007's *No Promises*, was made up of musical adaptations of well-known works by English-language poets. In 2008 she married the President of France, Nicolas Sarkozy.

6 Gitanes.

In 2017, German police were able to return Lennon's cigarette case containing Gitanes to Yoko Ono after recovering it from a thief. Both Gitanes and similar brand Gauloises were first developed before the First World War by the state-owned tobacco company and were packaged to reflect traditional patriotic values. In 2018 the two brands were at the centre of a proposal to ban them on the grounds that they were still seen by young people as the essence of cool.

7 Vienna and Düsseldorf.

8 'All You Need Is Love'.

In 1967 the Beatles had signed up to appear on the *Our World* TV broadcast which included contributions from all over the globe, and needed to come up with a song for the occasion. On the basis of it being the world's second favourite national anthem, George Martin suggested that the song 'All You Need Is Love' should begin with the opening bars of 'La Marseillaise'. Nobody pointed out that this song, far from being a hymn to peace, was first written to whip up the citizenry for war against Austria in 1792.

9 Héloïse Letissier.

She became famous as the leader of Christine and the Queens but now prefers to be known simply as Chris. The Guernsey-born footballer Matt Le Tissier played for England at under-21 and senior level between 1988 and 1997.

10 'Morning Train (Nine To Five)'.

Vartan's song is based on the tune and arrangement of the Sheena Easton hit and then veers off in another lyrical direction altogether.

'The nice thing about "All You Need Is Love" is that it cannot be misinterpreted.'

Brian Epstein

SCHOOL TRIP: LONDON

The Who at the exact centre of the world.

QUESTIONS

The citizens of London, much like New Yorkers and Parisians, have something of a superiority complex, taking little notice of anyone who does their city down because they genuinely don't understand anyone wanting to live anywhere else. Thus they think all the songs that weren't inspired by London ought to have been. Here are ten of them, all rooted in either a real or an imagined version of the great metropolis.

1 Was 'Itchycoo Park' inspired solely by the amount of dope the Small Faces had been smoking in 1967 or is it based on an actual London location?

2 Which celebrated progressive rock recording was inspired by a gangland quarrel settled in an ancient woodland on the edge of the capital?

3 Did a US president name his child after an upmarket district of south-west London referred to in a song by Joni Mitchell?

4 What's the link between Warren Zevon's 'Werewolves Of London' and the Everly Brothers' 'Crying In The Rain'?

5 What's the hit song named after the first London shopping street to be lit by electricity?

6 What was the 2006 hit record the title of which was pronounced 'London' but wasn't spelled that way?

7 What was the international hit single that was inspired by the experience of watching an amateur band play in a pub not far from where, four hundred years earlier, playwright Christopher Marlowe had been killed in an argument over a bill?

8 Which famous album covers were photographed in the following London postal codes?

   a) W1B 4BH
   b) SW8 5BP
   c) E4 8SJ
   d) NW8 0AH
   e) EC1V 8EN

9 Which famous song from the 1960s was inspired by an assignation with a photographer's wife in an apartment at Emperor's Gate, Kensington?

10 Were the couple Terry and Julie mentioned in the Kinks song 'Waterloo Sunset' actually based on Terence Stamp and Julie Christie, at the time starring in *Far from the Madding Crowd*?

ANSWERS

1 There is rarely one simple, literal explanation behind a song. 'Itchycoo Park' may propose a demi-paradise where one can blow one's mind while also feeding the ducks with a bun but it was said to be inspired by a place in Manor Park, east London, close to where the band had all grown up, a place known for its stinging nettles. It also owed something to the Small Faces' habit at the time of describing anything they didn't like as 'icky-bo'. There may also have been a subliminal element. They might not have been aware that the park alongside Christ Church, Spitalfields had long been known as 'Itchy Park' in reference to the down-and-outs who slept there. The American writer Jack London wrote about his visit there in *The People of the Abyss* (1903).

2 'The Battle Of Epping Forest'.

This track from the 1973 Genesis album *Selling England By The Pound* was inspired by a newspaper story Peter Gabriel read at the time about criminal gangs from the East End who would use the ancient parkland as a place to settle their differences. Forty-five years after the Genesis song it remains a popular site for gangland executions, its boggy ground being perfect for the disposal of inconvenient cadavers.

3 Not really.

The Clintons named their daughter Chelsea, who was born in 1980, after the 1968 Joni Mitchell song 'Chelsea Morning', which had always been a favourite of theirs. However, the song was actually inspired by the Chelsea district in New York where Mitchell was living at the time and mentions the light refracting from the mobile she had made herself from coloured glass she had found in an alley in Philadelphia. It's nothing to do with the Chelsea in London.

4 The link is that Phil Everly was watching the 1935 horror film *Werewolf of London* when he got the idea that his friend Warren Zevon should write a dance craze song with the same name. Zevon did so, never thinking it would amount to anything more than a joke. However, his friend Jackson Browne started playing the song live and so he was eventually forced to record it himself. Notwithstanding this he refused to take it seriously and was insulted when the record company put it out as a single, and deeply ambivalent when it became the biggest hit of his career. Appearing on *The Larry Sanders Show* in 1993 he said, 'Every show I do I play "Werewolves Of London" and it's driving me fucking crazy.'

5 'Electric Avenue' by Eddy Grant.

Electric Avenue in Brixton was built in 1888 and provided shoppers with the additional convenience of an iron and glass canopy to keep the rain off as they shopped. Grant's 1982 hit record was written in response to the riots that had devastated the area in 1980.

6 'LDN' by Lily Allen.

The song climbed to number six in 2006.

7 'Sultans Of Swing' by Dire Straits.

Mark Knopfler and John Illsley of the unsigned Dire Straits had seen a semi-pro band of middle-aged men who performed under the name the Sultans of Swing in a pub in Deptford. Deptford was the site of Marlowe's still-disputed murder in 1593.

8
a) *The Rise And Fall Of Ziggy Stardust And The Spiders From Mars* by David Bowie, which was shot in Heddon Street, just off Regent Street
b) Pink Floyd's *Animals*, featuring Battersea Power Station
c) Blur's *Parklife*, which was shot at Walthamstow Stadium
d) *Abbey Road*, shot in the road of the same name in St John's Wood
e) *Original Pirate Material* by the Streets, which shows Kestrel House on the City Road in Islington

9 'Norwegian Wood (This Bird Has Flown)'.

The song was written by John Lennon following a brief liaison with a former Pirelli calendar model who was married to a photographer who worked with the Beatles. The couple shared a flat in the same block as Lennon and his wife Cynthia.

10

No.

Well, if it makes you happy to visualize Terence Stamp and Julie Christie you're of course encouraged to do so, but according to Ray Davies they were never in his mind when he wrote the song. Closer to his thoughts was a friend of his called Terry who was moving away with his girlfriend to start a new life. Davies has also subsequently said that the song was originally called 'Liverpool Sunset', which would not have been anything like as euphonious.

Bluesman Pink Anderson, whose name lives on.

GENERAL STUDIES

QUESTIONS

One of the great things about being a pop star is that on day one you're allowed to give yourself a name and nobody seriously expects it to make a lick of sense. What it should do is make a good quiz question. Here are ten.

1 This name was first used in Britain by a psychedelic duo of the late sixties. It was later adopted far more successfully by America's most popular band of the late eighties and early nineties. What's the name?

2 One of Britain's most popular singles bands of the seventies acquired their name from their manager's secretary's habit of giving names to all her fashion accessories. Who were they?

3 One of the planet's most enduringly popular bands got their name from the surnames of the members of their rhythm section. Over the last fifty years scores of other members have been and gone but they and their name remain in place. Who are the band?

4 Some band names don't take off the first time they're used. This name was first used in Britain by a band with Mary Hopkin and Peter Skellern in their ranks who formed and broke up in 1984. The name was later taken up and used by which popular group of the 1990s?

5 Which of Britain's best-known and longest-established acts was named by fusing the names of two obscure bluesmen from the area of the Eastern Seaboard known as the Piedmont?

6 This name was first used by a cult favourite psychedelic band who broke up in San Francisco in 1969. It was later adopted by a band formed in the West Midlands in 1989 who are still playing today. What is it?

7 Who was given his stage name after somebody reversed the spelling of his actual first name?

8 Which rock icons carried these unlikely middle names?

  a) Frederick Joseph
  b) Allen
  c) Lynn
  d) Louise
  e) Zenon

9 Which four artists promoted themselves under the following modest subtitles?

  a) King of Pop
  b) Queen of Soul
  c) Minister of Super-heavy Funk
  d) the Genius

10 The following musicians were all nicknamed after which creatures?

    a) John Entwistle of the Who
    b) Derek Dick of Marillion
    c) Bob Hite of Canned Heat

ANSWERS

1 Nirvana.

The original Nirvana was created by Patrick Campbell-Lyons and Alex Spyropoulos in London in the mid-sixties and their early recordings on the Island label had many admirers. By the time the Kurt Cobain-led band of the same name became the most popular act on the planet in the early nineties the original group had re-formed. They eventually reached an agreement with Cobain about the name and shelved their plans for releasing an album called *Nirvana Sings Nirvana*.

2 Slade.

The group, who were initially known as the 'N Betweens, changed their name in 1969 at the insistence of the head of their record label who had a secretary with the strange habit of giving her accessories names. Her handbag was known as Ambrose and her shoes were known as Slade: the band changed their name first to Ambrose Slade and then to the more pithy Slade.

3 Fleetwood Mac.

The band, who were formed in London in 1967 and are still on tour over fifty years later, were named after their least prominent members, drummer

Mick Fleetwood and bassist John McVie. Owning a band's name is the thing that matters most in the long run. Actually being the name is even better.

4 Oasis.

First the name of a short-lived would-be supergroup from 1984 whose members included Skellern, Hopkin and Julian Lloyd Webber, the slightly better-known Oasis acquired the name in 1991 when Liam Gallagher saw a tour poster that referred to the Oasis Leisure Centre in Swindon.

5 Pink Floyd.

The young Syd Barrett noticed the names of Pink Anderson and Floyd Council in the sleeve notes of a 1962 album by Blind Boy Fuller. He took the two first names and combined them, accidentally happening on precisely the other-worldly vibe that seemed to suit his band, who began calling themselves the Pink Floyd Sound in 1965, abbreviating their name to Pink Floyd from the following year.

6 The Charlatans.

The first group were from northern California and became popular in San Francisco in 1967 but broke up two years later. Their drummer was Dan Hicks, who went on to lead his own band. The name was taken up in 1989 by a Tim Burgess-led group that went on to have hits in the UK during the 1990s.

7 Midge Ure.

His actual name is James Ure. When he joined his first professional band Salvation in Glasgow in 1971 they already had a James in the band and therefore it was suggested his diminutive Jim should be reversed to make 'Mij', which eventually became Midge.

8
a) Bruce Frederick Joseph Springsteen
b) Robert Allen Zimmerman (Bob Dylan)
c) Stephanie Lynn Nicks (Stevie Nicks)
d) Madonna Louise Ciccone
e) Robert Frederick Zenon Geldof (Zenon was the name of Bob's Belgian grandfather)

9
a) Michael Jackson, who was always bothered by the fact that although he had sold records in quantities nobody had ever dreamed of before he still didn't have an honorific title like other superstars did. Therefore he coined the idea of being the King of Pop and insisted he be known as such.
b) Aretha Franklin, who actually usurped the title Queen of Soul from Etta James, who had an album out under that name as early as 1964, when Aretha was still ploughing a furrow down the middle of the road on Columbia.
c) James Brown, who used to be announced onstage by a list of titles including Hardest Working Man in Show Business and the Godfather of Soul.

d) Ray Charles. Atlantic Records promoted him as the Genius from early on in his career, following 1959's *The Genius Of Ray Charles* with *The Genius Sings The Blues*, *The Genius After Hours* and numerous other spins on the same idea.

10
a) John Entwistle was known as the Ox
b) Derek Dick was Fish
c) Bob Hite was the Bear

Freddie Mercury:
full of Eastern
promise.

GEOGRAPHY

QUESTIONS

There are many cases where the demands of the pop song have ridden roughshod over the facts of geography and blithely carried on in the hope nobody would notice. For instance, the Band Aid record incorrectly predicted that there wouldn't be any snow in Africa that Christmas, despite the clearly visible evidence to the contrary provided by the snow that is always on the top of Mount Kilimanjaro. The Chattanooga Choo Choo didn't actually leave from track 29. Despite what Paper Lace argued in 'The Night Chicago Died', the lakeside city has no east side. But for every case where pop music has played fast and loose with the facts of the physical world there are many others where it has sent us to the map drawer to find out more.

1 Which famous rock standard was inspired by what the band could see when they were looking across Lake Geneva on a fateful day in 1971?

2 Only two British groups have seen their first three singles go to number one. Who were they, and what fluvial song did they have in common?

3 Who was born furthest east – Cliff Richard, Joe Strummer or Freddie Mercury?

4 Which river in Ohio, once so polluted that it was declared a fire risk, inspired songs by Randy Newman and R.E.M.?

5 Led Zeppelin's 'When The Levee Breaks' is a remake of a song by Memphis Minnie. What historic natural disaster does that song describe?

6 What geographical feature did Dr Feelgood have in common with Level 42?

7 How many rivers were there in Babylon, and can you name them?

8 Chuck Berry's song 'Promised Land' describes a cross-country journey that ends in Los Angeles. Where does the journey begin?

9 Which of Van Morrison's signature songs invokes the actual name of a river?

10 Name the three countries administering the geographical region that provides the name for one of Led Zeppelin's most celebrated songs.

ANSWERS

1 'Smoke On The Water'.

The members of Deep Purple were in Geneva to record their new album in 1971 when they saw the casino in Montreux catch fire during a concert by Frank Zappa. This inspired them to write 'Smoke On The Water', which became their signature song.

2 Gerry and the Pacemakers and Frankie Goes to Hollywood.

Gerry and the Pacemakers saw their first three hits go to the top of the chart in 1963-4, and Frankie Goes to Hollywood matched the feat twenty years later. On the B-side of Frankie's first, 'Relax', was their version of Gerry's 'Ferry Cross The Mersey'. Both groups of course came from Liverpool.

3 Cliff Richard.

Joe Strummer (real name John Mellor) was born in Ankara, Turkey, in 1952. His father was employed by the British Foreign Service at the time. Freddie Mercury (real name Farrokh Bulsara) was born in Zanzibar in 1946, where his Indian father was working for the British Colonial Office. Cliff Richard (real name Harry Webb) was born in Lucknow, India, in 1940, where his father worked for the Indian Railways.

4 The Cuyahoga.

The river was so badly polluted that in 1969 it did actually catch fire. This event, coming at a time when concern about pollution was on the rise, made it infamous across the United States. Randy Newman's 1972 song 'Burn On' extended that infamy and took it round the world. The R.E.M. song 'Cuyahoga', which featured on their 1986 album *Lifes Rich Pageant*, proposes building a new America in the place where it had all apparently gone wrong.

5 The Great Mississippi Flood of 1927.

'When The Levee Breaks' describes what happened when the Mississippi broke its banks as a result of this disastrous flood. The levee that bordered the river was meant to keep its water from flooding the homes and farms of the people who lived either side, the majority of whom were poor African-Americans. Two hundred thousand people were displaced and forced to live in relief camps.

6 Islands.

Both bands were formed on islands: Dr Feelgood came from Canvey Island and Level 42 from the Isle of Wight.

7 Two, the Tigris and the Euphrates.

The 'Rivers of Babylon', where, according to the psalm and song popularized by Boney M., the children of Israel sat down and wept as they remembered Zion, were the Tigris and the Euphrates, which flow through Turkey, Syria and Iraq.

8 Norfolk, Virginia.

In the last line of 'Promised Land' the hero places a call to the folks back home to say he's arrived. The line, which is one of the neatest lyrical constructs in rock, goes 'Los Angeles, give me Norfolk, Virginia, Tidewater four ten oh nine'.

9 'Into The Mystic'.

The song is on Van's 1970 album *Moondance*. The Belfast musician was living and working in Massachusetts at the time. The Mystic River lies to the north of Boston and flows from the Lower Mystic Lake to the Charles River. The name derives from a Native American word 'missi-tuk', which means 'big river'.

10 The three countries administering Kashmir, which lends its name to a song on Led Zeppelin's *Physical Graffiti*, are India, Pakistan and China.

GERMAN

Nena in the act of making the wall come down.

QUESTIONS

In the late sixties the very idea that Germany would ever be fashionable in pop music terms would have seemed laughable. Germany's major contribution to the British charts in those days seemed to be Horst Jankowski's 'A Walk In The Black Forest'. Its most significant city was Hamburg on the grounds that this was where the Beatles had honed their act. Not any longer.

1 The David Bowie albums *Low, Heroes* and *Lodger* are often referred to as his Berlin trilogy. Why is this a misleading description of them?

2 The one and only time Elvis Presley set foot on British soil was during a brief stopover on a flight back from Germany to the United States at the end of his service in the army. Where in the UK did he set down?

3 The Beatles rerecorded two of their big hits in German-language versions. Which two hits?

4 Die Toten Hosen have been one of Germany's most popular acts since 1984. What does the name mean in English, both literally and metaphorically?

5 The lead singer of which Californian band, who recorded the definitive version of one of the most enduring anthems of the late sixties, was born in East Prussia during the Second World War and was taken west by his mother to flee the advancing Russians?

6 How is Christa Päffgen better known in the USA and England?

7 In which German city did Freddie Mercury reside and do his most energetic partying in the mid-1980s?

8 When David Bowie and Brian Eno were recording in Germany the latter brought a new, German-made record into the studio and promised 'this will change the sound of clubbing music for many years to come'. What was the record?

9 Who were the German duo who returned their Grammys following a scandal about whether or not they actually sang on their hit recordings?

10 The list of the all-time top-selling albums in Germany is dominated by anglophone performers such as Abba, Phil Collins, Tracy Chapman and Genesis, but the number one is by a German artist. Who is that artist?

ANSWERS

1 They weren't all made in Berlin.

Although Bowie was a resident of Berlin in the mid-seventies at the time he made these records and they were widely praised for their bleak chic, *Low* was actually recorded in France and most of *Lodger* was done in Switzerland, always a popular spot for millionaires keen to minimize their tax liability.

2 Prestwick.

The plane taking Elvis Presley back to the United States at the end of his military service in Germany on 3 March 1960 touched down at Prestwick Airport in Scotland, which was then the home of the 1631st Air Base Squadron of the USAF Military Air Transport Service. In the few hours Elvis was there he posed for pictures with fans and talked to local press. He never returned to Europe.

3 'She Loves You' and 'I Want To Hold Your Hand'.

In January 1964, just before they made their first visit to the United States which would see them transformed into a planetary sensation, the Beatles reluctantly went into a studio in Paris to record German-language vocals for 'She Loves You' ('Sie Liebt Dich') and 'I Want To Hold Your Hand' ('Komm, Gib Mir Deine Hand') at the insistence of their German record company Odeon, who argued that the German public would never buy their records unless they were done in German. The Beatles never made this kind of concession again.

4 The literal translation of Die Toten Hosen is 'The Dead Trousers'. It's actually a metaphor that is used to describe erectile dysfunction.

5 John Kay of Steppenwolf.

Joachim Krauledat was born in 1944 in East Prussia, at the time an outpost of the German Reich stranded between Poland and Lithuania. His father, a German soldier, died before he was born and his mother fled with him to get away from the advancing Russians. When he and his family moved to Canada in 1958 he became John Kay. He joined a band called the Sparrows in 1965. The Sparrows became Steppenwolf and went on to have major success with songs such as 'Magic Carpet Ride', 'The Pusher' and the definitive rebel music anthem 'Born To Be Wild'.

6 Nico.

Christa Päffgen was born in 1938 in Cologne, grew up during the war and its aftermath, left school at thirteen and soon got work as a model under the name Nico. She moved to New York in the early 1960s and began singing in public. At Andy Warhol's insistence she was introduced into the Velvet Underground in 1967. She died in 1988 at the age of forty-nine.

7 Munich.

Queen initially went to the south German city to record an album but it eventually became their de facto base, thanks to the fact that Mercury loved spending time in the city's gay scene. He liked it because, as Mercury's friend Paul Gambaccini recalled, 'New York and Munich were the capitals of anonymous, one-time-only sex.'

8 'I Feel Love' by Donna Summer.

The record that Brian Eno said would change music was recorded in Munich in 1977 by Donna Summer with production from Giorgio Moroder. It is widely regarded as the departure point for all electronic dance music.

9 Milli Vanilli.

The duo had major worldwide hits with 'Girl You Know It's True' and 'Baby Don't Forget My Number' in the late 1980s. During this time there was widespread speculation that Fab Morvan and Rob Pilatus could not have sung on their hits. This culminated in 1990 with actions being brought on behalf of members of the public who claimed they had bought their records believing the people fronting them on TV were the people singing on them. The duo returned the Grammys they had won and tried unsuccessfully to relaunch their career under their individual names. Rob Pilatus died in Frankfurt in 1998.

10 Herbert Grönemeyer.

Germany's most popular musician and number-one album seller is best known in the rest of the world as the war correspondent in the movie *Das Boot*.

HISTORY

Abba: not the most reliable source of historical information.

History I

QUESTIONS

No subject category has been more energetically mined for ideas for songs or self-aggrandizing album cover treatments than history, which has been ransacked for inspiration down the years by musicians who often weren't as concerned with factual accuracy as they might have been. Here are ten cases of history being put to use in pursuit of pop success.

1 Who was the British prime minister of the nineteenth century who gave his name to a psychedelic album that went on to become a big hit? And while you're about it, can you name the twentieth-century prime minister whose surname is also the title of an album by Everything But The Girl?

2 The opening line of Abba's 'Waterloo' states that this was where Napoleon surrendered. In which modern country is the battlefield of Waterloo situated?

3 Which song by a Scottish group, inspired by the Enniskillen bombing of 1987, reached number one in the UK in 1989?

4 Deep Purple wrote a song called 'Jack Ruby'. Who did Jack Ruby kill?

5 Which of these three Neil Young songs was not about an actual historical figure: 'Cortez The Killer', 'Pocahontas', 'The Emperor Of Wyoming'?

6 Who is the Scottish band named after a figure whose assassination triggered the series of events that led to the outbreak of the First World War?

7 Name the bands who took their names from:

a) the 1825 rebellion against the Russian tsar led by army officers

b) the radical movement for people's rights that emerged in England at the end of the Civil War

c) the revolutionaries of the 1871 Paris Commune

8 Both the Bee Gees and Stephen Stills released albums named after the sites of famous battles. What are they?

9 A famous photograph of American soldiers raising a flag was pastiched on the covers of albums by Funkadelic, Canned Heat and Uriah Heep among many others. Where in the world was that flag originally raised?

10 The cover of *Deep Purple In Rock* is a pastiche of the sculptures of the faces of American presidents which are carved into Mount Rushmore in South Dakota. Who are the four presidents depicted on the original memorial?

ANSWERS

1 Benjamin Disraeli.

The 1967 Cream LP *Disraeli Gears* was so called thanks to a mishearing during a conversation which referred to derailleur gears on a bicycle. The 1984 Everything But The Girl album *Eden* had nothing to do with the post-war prime minister Anthony Eden, whose primary distinction was that he was the most handsome man who ever held the office.

2 Belgium.

The battlefield of Waterloo lies ten miles south of Brussels in what is now the nation state of Belgium. At the time of the battle in 1815 Belgium didn't yet exist and it was part of the United Kingdom of the Netherlands. Despite what Björn and Benny wrote, Napoleon did not actually surrender at Waterloo. He retreated after the arrival of the Prussians and, after failing to rally support in Paris, abdicated four days after the battle.

3 'Belfast Child' by Simple Minds.

The bombing by the Provisional IRA of a Remembrance Day parade in Enniskillen killed eleven and injured many more and was to prove a turning point in Northern Ireland's road to peace. Jim Kerr of Simple Minds was watching news footage of the devastation and had the idea to adapt the traditional melody 'She Moved Through The Fair' for a new song which he called 'Belfast Child'. This reached number one in the UK in February 1989.

4 Lee Harvey Oswald.

Jack Ruby was the Dallas nightclub owner who shot and killed the man accused of the assassination of John F. Kennedy, in the basement of the Dallas Police Headquarters on 24 November 1963, as Oswald was being transferred to another jail. The involvement of Ruby, who had mob connections, in an action which meant that Oswald could never give evidence in court served to thicken the cloud of speculation about conspiracies that has dogged the event to the present day.

5 'The Emperor Of Wyoming'.

Hernán Cortés was a Spanish conquistador of the sixteenth century whose occupation of Mexico led to the massacre of thousands of local leaders. Pocahontas was the daughter of a Native American chieftain who was captured and held for ransom by English forces in the early seventeenth century; she died in England and was buried in Gravesend. 'The Emperor Of Wyoming' is the opening instrumental on Young's first album and does not refer to any actual figure, living or dead. It is so called merely in order to encourage speculation and to provide material for those compiling quizzes fifty years after its release.

6 Franz Ferdinand.

The band formed in Glasgow in 2002 and took their name from a racehorse called Archduke Ferdinand which had won the Northumberland Plate in 2001. This beast had been named in honour of the heir to the Austrian throne who was shot in Sarajevo in 1914.

7 a) the Decemberists
b) the Levellers
c) the Communards

8 Trafalgar and Manassas.

In 1971 the Bee Gees released *Trafalgar* which had a painting of an action of the 1805 naval battle on its cover. In 1972 Stephen Stills released *Manassas* and lined up with his fellow band members on the platform of the station in Virginia where not one but two bloody battles (the First and Second Battles of Bull Run) took place during the American Civil War.

9 Iwo Jima, Japan.

The image of six US Marines struggling to bring a flag into an upright position, which was pastiched for Funkadelic's *One Nation Under A Groove*, Canned Heat's *Future Blues* and Uriah Heep's *Conquest*, was taken on Mount Suribachi on the island of Iwo Jima during one of the key battles that took place towards the end of the Second World War.

10 George Washington, Thomas Jefferson, Theodore Roosevelt and Abraham Lincoln. A petition to add Donald Trump's face to the mountain has not yet reached its target number of signatures.

History II

QUESTIONS

The old journalistic saw holds that if it's a story it isn't true, and if it's true it isn't a story. Rock & roll owes as much to the enduring power of mythology as it does to the backbeat. Here are ten questions about legends, or the legends we believe to be historical facts.

1 What do the Woodstock Festival and the Glastonbury Festival have in common?

2 What were the clues on the cover of *Abbey Road* allegedly pointing to the fact that Paul McCartney was dead?

3 Rick Wakeman made three albums – *The Six Wives Of Henry VIII*, *King Arthur And The Knights Of The Round Table* and *Journey To The Centre Of The Earth* – that made use of popular historical themes. But which ones are historically accurate?

4 Which German group took their name from a figure of the German Renaissance who inspired scores of works of fiction about a man exchanging his soul for earthly success?

5 How many of these Bob Dylan songs are about mythical figures?

    a) 'John Wesley Harding'
    b) 'Isis'
    c) 'Joey'
    d) 'Who Killed Davey Moore?'

6 The album released in late 1974 by Van Morrison is called *Veedon Fleece*. What is the Veedon Fleece?

7 Which British magician and occultist was mentioned in the lyrics of the David Bowie song 'Quicksand' and features as one of the characters on the cover of *Sgt. Pepper's Lonely Hearts Club Band*?

8 What model of car did Keith Moon once drive into a swimming pool?

9 What's the movie you're supposed to watch while listening to *The Dark Side Of The Moon* in order to have special secrets revealed to you?

10 Charles Manson was one of the many Hollywood hopefuls who auditioned for the Monkees. True or false?

ANSWERS

1 Neither of them took place at the town they're named after.

The Woodstock Festival had to be relocated at the last minute to Bethel in New York State, and the Glastonbury Festival takes place twenty-three miles away at Worthy Farm. The name has been in use since 1971 because it was easier to market.

2 The fact that his feet were bare while the rest of the band were shod supposedly indicated that McCartney was the corpse in a funeral procession. The registration number of the VW parked in the road, 28IF, was taken to refer to the age he would have been had he lived. Some also said that the fact that McCartney, a famous left-hander, had his cigarette in his right hand in the picture indicated he was being played by an impostor.

3 Only *The Six Wives Of Henry VIII*.

King Arthur derives from Anglo-Saxon legends (the full title of Wakeman's album is *The Myths And Legends Of King Arthur And The Knights Of The Round Table*). *Journey To The Centre Of The Earth* was based on a Jules Verne novel.

4 Faust.

The group, who formed in 1971, were named after the semi-mythological figure who was in turn based on the fifteenth-century alchemist and magician Johann Faust.

5 Only b) 'Isis'.

Gunfighter John Wesley Harding, gangster Joey Gallo and prizefighter Davey Moore all walked the earth, even though Dylan may have been guilty of increasing the colour and contrast on their real-life careers in order to make them serve his purpose. For Isis, however, he was reaching back into Egyptian mythology where this mythical figure played an important role in ushering the dead into the afterlife.

6 There is no Veedon Fleece. There never was a Veedon Fleece. They are simply a couple of words that popped into Van's head when he was singing. 'I haven't a clue what the title means,' he says.

7 Aleister Crowley.

Crowley, who spent much of his life blurring the line between reality and mysticism, appears second from the left on the top row of the cover of *Sgt. Pepper*.

8 None, because he didn't drive.

The version of this myth that has gone into history has Keith driving a Rolls-Royce into a swimming pool. There were two incidents which, according to Pete Townshend, were conflated into one. In the first the brake was left off a Lincoln Continental which then rolled into an empty swimming pool. In the second the band refused to allow Moon to charge his new English car to the band so he parked it in a muddy pond at the bottom of his garden and demanded it be picked up.

9 *The Wizard of Oz.*

Only on American radio could somebody have cooked up the story that if you watch *The Wizard of Oz* while listening to *The Dark Side Of The Moon* then all manner of spooky synchronicities will be revealed to you. It is of course a myth.

10 False.

Manson was in prison at the time auditions were held for the Monkees.

'You want the truth? You couldn't afford me.'

Keith Moon

HOME ECONOMICS

The none-more-demanding David Lee Roth.

QUESTIONS

In the days when this subject was known as 'Domestic Science' it was largely confined to matters of the kitchen and was considered to be the exclusive domain of the female sex. Now we know that it is everyone's concern and encompasses anything that pertains to where and how we live and how we feed ourselves.

1 Which 1995 number one hit was inspired by the group's former manager's wish to escape the music business rat race and buy a house outside the city?

2 Which colour sweets had to be removed from the bowls of M&M's provided in Van Halen's dressing room according to the stipulations of their contract with the promoter?

3 What was the Beatles' favourite drink until Bob Dylan turned them on to marijuana?

4 Which high-profile rock star says he only eats bread, potatoes, pasta and nuts and recently said, 'I'm absolutely hopeless when I'm handed a menu in a restaurant. I go directly to the Kiddies' Meals. If I find baked beans then the night is a huge success'?

5 Which guitar player and hunting enthusiast wrote a cookery book called *Kill It & Grill It*?

6 Which guitarist and songwriter dedicated his 1980 solo album to Rémy Martin Cognac 'for saving my life by making the stuff so bloody expensive'?

7 Who famously said, 'What we have in mind is breakfast in bed for four hundred thousand,' and where did he say it?

8 All these acts made albums named after meals: Ry Cooder, Supertramp, Cat Stevens, Black Uhuru. Place them in the order the meals would be served during the day.

9 All these hit records were made by bands with foodstuffs in their names. Who are the bands?
   a) 'When Love Breaks Down'
   b) 'Since Yesterday'
   c) 'I Had Too Much To Dream (Last Night)'
   d) '2 Become 1'

10 Bob Dylan has recently developed a collection of American whiskeys that are marketed under what name?

ANSWERS

1 'Country House' by Blur.

The song was inspired by former manager Dave Balfe's plan to withdraw from the business to a house in the country. His plan was to explore various creative avenues, none of which actually panned out. Meanwhile *The Great Escape*, the album from which the song came, was such a success that Balfe was tempted to return to the rat race as a record company executive.

2 The brown ones.

Van Halen's 1982 rider specified that they have 'M&M's (WARNING: ABSOLUTELY NO BROWN ONES)'. This clause was included simply to stress how particular the band were and how their people would come down hard on any promoter who failed to come up to code in any respect that actually mattered.

3 Scotch and Coke.

All through the madness of Beatlemania John, Paul, George and Ringo sustained themselves on a beverage few people drink nowadays, a libation the very thought of which is enough to turn most stomachs. 'Until Bob Dylan turned us on to marijuana,' recalled

Paul McCartney in the *Anthology* TV documentary, 'we were Scotch and Coke men.'

4 Morrissey.

The same Morrissey who won't allow meat products to be sold in venues where he's performing. He added, 'If you ever bring me out to dinner it's important that you also bring a toaster.'

5 Ted Nugent.

Nugent and his wife Shemane published *Kill It & Grill It* in 2005. In it they share their preferred way of serving wild boar, pheasant, buffalo and venison.

6 Pete Townshend.

The sardonic thank you to Rémy Martin was among the credits on Townshend's 1980 solo album *Empty Glass*.

7 Wavy Gravy, at the Woodstock Festival.

In the film *Woodstock*, shot in 1969, hippy activist Wavy Gravy takes the microphone and uses that line when announcing the catering arrangements his organization the Hog Farm and other similar cooperatives were aiming to provide for the masses stranded at the festival site without any means of sustenance. 'We must be in heaven, man,' he adds. 'There is always a little bit of heaven in a disaster area.'

8 Supertramp's *Breakfast In America*, Ry Cooder's *Paradise And Lunch*, Cat Stevens' *Tea For The Tillerman*, and Black Uhuru's *Guess Who's Coming To Dinner*.

9
a) Prefab Sprout
b) Strawberry Switchblade
c) the Electric Prunes
d) Spice Girls

10 Dylan's whiskeys are marketed under the name 'Heaven's Door'.

'A man is a success if he gets up in the morning and gets to bed at night, and in between he does what he wants to do.'

Bob Dylan

HOSPITALITY MANAGEMENT

And fans of Jimmy Buffett are known as what?

QUESTIONS

In which we delve into a field of study increasing numbers are pursuing as a vocational qualification. This subject heading covers everything from the hotels you stay in to the funfair rides you choose. It's an area in which we all have roughly the same experience but some of us have more opinions than others.

1 The Eagles, Wilco, the Doors and the Grateful Dead all made albums with the word 'hotel' in them. However, only one of them was a real hotel. Which one?

2 When Glasgow Rangers flew to Tel Aviv in 2007 to play a UEFA Cup tie, who was the celebrity pilot?

3 What's the song the band and fellow passengers sing along to on the bus as they bond after a fight in Cameron Crowe's 2000 film *Almost Famous*?

4 What cities are these famous rock & roll hotels situated in?

    a) the Gramercy Park Hotel
    b) the Sunset Marquis
    c) the Columbia Hotel

5 Which musical stars died in the following hotels in these years?

a) the Samarkand, London, 1970
b) the Hard Rock, Las Vegas, 2002
c) the Ritz-Carlton, Double Bay, Sydney, 1997
d) the Beverly Hilton, Beverly Hills, California, 2012

6 Which legendary band leader and singer used to frighten members of his band by insisting on taking the controls of their chartered plane as soon as it reached cruising altitude?

7 Name the band who've put on performances in the following exotic locations:

a) the Pyramids
b) Pompeii
c) 300 metres down in the North Sea
d) the Napa State Mental Hospital
e) the 144th floor of the CN Tower

8 What's the collective noun for fans of the following?

a) Jimmy Buffett
b) Bob Dylan
c) the Killers
d) Taylor Swift
e) Adele

9 Identify the noteworthy celebration from the situation these lyrics describe:

a) the birthday girl is in tears because Johnny left with Judy

b) the host invites you to help yourself to the Cokes in the icebox and the popcorn on the table

c) with all the wedding invitations sent, the young bride went away

10 What are the following acts welcoming us to?

a) Frankie Goes to Hollywood

b) Elvis Costello

c) Guns N' Roses

d) Public Enemy

ANSWERS

1 The Morrison Hotel.

The front cover picture of *Morrison Hotel*, the 1970 album by the Doors, was taken in an actual cheap rooming house of that name in downtown Los Angeles. The Eagles' *Hotel California* and the Grateful Dead's *From The Mars Hotel* were both fictions. Wilco's *Yankee Hotel Foxtrot* was based on a radio call sign.

2 Bruce Dickinson.

The Iron Maiden singer is a licensed commercial pilot, in which capacity he has flown football teams to overseas fixtures as well as transporting Iron Maiden and their equipment on tour.

3 'Tiny Dancer' by Elton John.

'Tiny Dancer' is from Elton John's 1971 album *Madman Across The Water*.

4 a) New York
b) Los Angeles
c) London

The Gramercy Park Hotel is in New York and was a magnet for bands on their way up. Nowadays, it can only be afforded by bands who are already on top. The Sunset Marquis (pronounced 'marquee') is in Hollywood. The Columbia Hotel in Lancaster Gate, London, used to be *the* rock & roll hotel in the early eighties.

5
a) Jimi Hendrix
b) John Entwistle
c) Michael Hutchence
d) Whitney Houston

6 Ray Charles.

Said Bobby Womack, who toured with him in the 1970s, 'As soon as we hit air, the buckle was off and Ray raced up the aisle towards the cockpit. I said, "Where's he going?" He never runs like that when he's going on stage to play the piano.'

7
a) the Grateful Dead played the Pyramids in Egypt in 1978
b) Pink Floyd played in the amphitheatre at Pompeii in 1972
c) Katie Melua played on a gas rig a thousand feet below sea level in 2006
d) the Cramps played the Napa State Mental Hospital in California in 1978
e) Spiritualized hold the record for the highest performance with their 1997 show on the 144th floor of the CN Tower in Toronto

8
a) Jimmy Buffett fans call themselves Parrotheads
b) hardcore Bob Dylan fans identify as Bobcats
c) fans of the Killers embrace the title Victims

d) Taylor Swift fans are Swifties

e) Adele fans are Daydreamers

9

a) 'It's My Party' by Lesley Gore

b) 'Having A Party' by Sam Cooke and the Pointer Sisters

c) '$1000 Wedding' by Gram Parsons

10

a) Frankie Goes to Hollywood sang 'Welcome to the Pleasuredome'

b) Elvis Costello sang 'Welcome to the Working Week'

c) Guns N' Roses sang 'Welcome to the Jungle'

d) Public Enemy sang 'Welcome to the Terrordome'

LAW

Elvis fails to spot open cell door.

QUESTIONS

Despite the undying allure of outlaw chic, it is important that rock fans are able to distinguish between right and wrong and, thanks to the many songs that have gone before, to understand the price they may have to pay should they personally transgress. This section deals with the handful of artists who have had their collar felt (or worse) and others who have simply sung about the perils of fighting the law and the likelihood that in many of those cases the law is apt to win.

1 Which of the following never did actual jail time: Hugh Cornwell, Johnny Cash, Chuck Berry, James Brown, the Notorious B.I.G.?

2 According to the lyrics of Elvis Presley's 'Jailhouse Rock', what did number forty-seven say to number three and why might it have met with the disapproval of the authorities at the time?

3 Which famous reggae hit was inspired by the artist's number in prison following a conviction in 1966 for possession of marijuana?

4 Alexander Minto Hughes had a series of reggae hits in the UK in the late sixties and early seventies under what legal title?

5 Which album sleeve featured a boxer, a Member of Parliament and two movie actors apparently caught in the spotlight during a prison break?

6 Three real-life criminal couples inspired three different songs by Bruce Springsteen, Georgie Fame and the Smiths. Who were they?

7 Genesis, Thin Lizzy and Black Sabbath all named albums after which specific crimes?

8 A band formed in east London in 1975 and named after a mythic torture device went on to become one of the UK's most popular exports. Can you name them?

9 When Mick Jagger and Keith Richards were being sent to prison in 1967 for possession of dangerous drugs, the editor of *The Times* wrote a sympathetic editorial headlined 'Who breaks a butterfly on a wheel?'. Who was that editor?

10 Who was the artist who was the intended victim of a bungled plot to murder her at her home in Devon in 2013?

ANSWERS

1 Johnny Cash.

His concerts at San Quentin and Folsom prisons, together with a few nights in the cooler here and there, may have helped carve out an image as one of nature's outlaws but in fact Cash was the only one of the list who never did actual jail time. Hugh Cornwell did time for drug offences, Chuck Berry for an offence under the Mann Act, James Brown for theft and then years later for assaulting a police officer, and the Notorious B.I.G., otherwise known as Christopher Wallace, for dealing crack cocaine.

2 Number forty-seven said to number three, 'You're the cutest jailbird I ever did see.'

In 1957, when the song was written, same-sex relationships were widely interpreted as a threat to the established order.

3 '54-46 That's My Number'.

This 1968 hit from Toots and the Maytals was inspired by frontman Toots Hibbert's time in chokey.

4 Judge Dread.

He was the artist behind such bawdy hits as 'Big Seven' and 'Y Viva Suspenders'. In the 1970s he had more reggae hits than any other artist, despite hailing from Kent rather than Kingston.

5 *Band On The Run.*

The cover of the 1973 album by Paul McCartney and Wings features Paul, Linda and Denny Laine along with six 'personalities': actors Christopher Lee and James Coburn, boxer John Conteh, Clement Freud MP, chat show host Michael Parkinson and musician Kenny Lynch.

6 Charlie Starkweather and Caril Ann Fugate; Bonnie Parker and Clyde Barrow; Ian Brady and Myra Hindley.

The Bruce Springsteen song 'Nebraska' was inspired by the story of Charlie Starkweather and his girl-friend Caril Ann Fugate who were tried for the kill-ings of eleven people in Nebraska and Wyoming in a month at the end of 1957. Georgie Fame was the most successful of many artists who decided it was OK to sing about the bank robbers and murderers Bonnie Parker and Clyde Barrow, who died in a police ambush in 1934. Fame's single 'The Ballad Of Bonnie And Clyde' reached the top of the charts in 1968. 'Suffer Little Children' was a 1984 song by the Smiths which was inspired by the murders of five Manchester children at the hands of 'Moors Murderers' Ian Brady and Myra Hindley.

7 Trespass, jailbreak and sabotage.

Trespass was the name of a 1970 album by Genesis, *Jailbreak* the name of a 1976 album by Thin Lizzy, and *Sabotage* the name of a 1975 album by Black Sabbath.

8 Iron Maiden.

There's some argument among historians as to whether the sarcophagus-like contraption found in various European museums was ever seriously used as an instrument of torture but the myth of the iron maiden was powerful enough for it to be taken up by the band, formed in Leyton in 1975.

9 William Rees-Mogg.

The man who wrote the *Times* editorial was the father of Jacob Rees-Mogg MP.

10 Joss Stone.

Two men from Manchester were found guilty of conspiracy to murder the singer at her home in Devon. One was jailed for life and the other for eighteen years.

'Sir, I guess there's just a meanness in this world.'

Bruce Springsteen in 'Nebraska'

LITERATURE

In the future, most bands will get their names from children's books.

QUESTIONS

In most bands there will be one member with a reputation for being something of a bookworm. This member will declare themselves as such by turning up at rehearsal with some dog-eared and soulful-looking paperback protruding from their back pocket. They will not always have read it. Listed below are ten bands who owe their names to the fact that one member occasionally went to the library. Can you identify them?

1 Who were the band who named themselves after a fictional pop group in Anthony Burgess's 1962 novel *A Clockwork Orange*, a group described as being at number four in the charts at the time with a song called 'Inside'?

2 Which band took their name from a novel originally published in French in 1956 under the title *La Chute*?

3 Which band named themselves after a spoiled brat in a book by Roald Dahl?

4 Which band took their name from the title of a book, first published in the US in 1963, whose cover breathlessly announced it as 'a documentary on the sexual corruption of our age, it is a must for every thinking adult'?

5 Which band, formed in New York in 1969, took their name from the title of a book, published in 1925, which D. H. Lawrence had described at the time as 'the best modern book about New York'?

6 Which British band, who up until that point had been known as Daddy, adopted their name in 1970 from the title of a book by a Welsh author which had been first published in 1908 with a preface by George Bernard Shaw?

7 Which American act took their name from an intimate device mentioned in a book published amid some controversy in Paris in 1959?

8 Which British band took their name from a book of poems by Philip Horky called *Child's Reflections*?

9 Who were the Irish band who took their name from a childhood gang referred to in Woody Guthrie's autobiography *Bound for Glory*?

10 Who are the American band, formed in 1992, who took their name from a passage in a story by Virginia Woolf entitled *The Mark on the Wall*?

ANSWERS

1 Heaven 17.

'Heaven Seventeen' are one of a list of bands in the novel being enthused about by teenage girls in a record shop. Heaven 17 was the name adopted by Martyn Ware and Ian Craig Marsh when they peeled off from the Human League in 1980 to form their own group.

2 The Fall.

'The Fall' is the literal translation of *La Chute*, by Albert Camus.

3 Veruca Salt.

Veruca Salt are an American alternative rock band formed in 1992. The original Veruca Salt was a character in *Charlie and the Chocolate Factory*, the heiress to the Salt nut fortune who has evidently been spoiled by her wealthy parents.

4 The Velvet Underground.

Michael Leigh's book *The Velvet Underground* was the best-seller that heralded 'the sexual revolution'. The name of the book was borrowed in 1965 by John Cale and Lou Reed for their new group. In Britain, the book was published under the nothing-like-as-catchy name *Bizarre Sex Underground*.

5 The Manhattan Transfer.

The vocal group got their name from the John Dos Passos novel of the same title, which was hailed as one of the first books to successfully reflect the experience of living in New York in the 1920s, at a time when its population was exploding.

6 Supertramp.

They took their name from the book *The Autobiography of a Super-Tramp* by the Welsh writer W. H. Davies. It described his wanderings in Britain and the United States, travels that were largely subsidized by begging.

7 Steely Dan.

The William Burroughs novel *The Naked Lunch* was published in Paris in 1959, in the days when accounts of the sexual adventures of heroin users could only be published in that city. In a book not short on controversy, the line 'Mary is strapping on a rubber penis' nonetheless stood out for the young Walter Becker and Donald Fagen. 'Steely Dan III from Yokohama,' Mary goes on to explain before describing the unfortunate fates of its two predecessors. Becker and Fagen decided that this would serve as the name for their new group.

8 Coldplay.

The subtitle of the book of poems known as *Child's Reflections* was 'Cold Play'. The two words were combined to make the name of the band, which had been formerly known as Pectoralz and Starfish.

9 The Boomtown Rats.

In Guthrie's 1943 autobiography he writes about how the discovery of oil transformed his home town, Okemah in Oklahoma, into a boom town. Suddenly the place was full of chancers intent on making their fortunes. Meanwhile, their children ran wild. Guthrie, who was one of them, describes a pitched battle between two rival gangs of children who turned water tanks into weapons. Victory was announced thus: 'Hooray fer th' tanks! / Hooray fer th' tanks! / That'll teach a lesson / To th' boom town rats!'

Bob Geldof had read the book and he suggested that as a name this would be an improvement on the previous Nightlife Thugs.

10 Modest Mouse.

Published in 1917, *The Mark on the Wall* was Woolf's first short story. In it she refers to the 'modest mouse-coloured people, who believe genuinely that they dislike to hear their own praises'. This sentence was adapted into the name Modest Mouse for the rock band formed in Washington State in 1992.

MATHEMATICS

When it came to maths Sam Cooke's knowledge was patchy.

QUESTIONS

The first songs we ever learn as children lean heavily on numbers. There were ten in the bed. The animals went in two by two. Five little ducks went swimming one day. Ten green bottles were standing on a wall. In grown-up popular song, numbers continue to play an important role. This particularly applies to Americans, whose cities are organized on grids reliant on numbers, exemplified in 'Positively Fourth Street', '53rd and 3rd', 'Across 110th Street' and hundreds of other songs. Finally there's the poignant arithmetic of romance, or its absence, in which one is the loneliest number, it takes two to make a dream come true, and the sight of three cigarettes in the ashtray rarely augurs well. This round is all about numbers, from those which simply landed in songs because they provided a handy rhyme to those which may be more significant than you might think.

1 How many Vestal Virgins were leaving for the coast in the 1967 Procol Harum hit 'A Whiter Shade Of Pale'?

2 How high does Canadian singer-songwriter Feist count in her 2007 hit '1234'?

3 How many numbers does Jonathan Richman count out at the beginning of his 1977 hit 'Roadrunner'?

4 What is De La Soul's 'Magic Number'?

5 In Sam Cooke's 1960 hit 'Wonderful World' he lists two branches of mathematics that he doesn't claim to know much about. What are they?

6 Which veteran British progressive act, formed in Manchester in 1967 and named after a piece of electrical equipment, made an album called *A Grounding In Numbers* in 2011, inspired in part by the equation known to mathematicians as Euler's Identity?

7 Did 10cc really get their name from the volume of the average male ejaculation?

8 Which Bob Dylan song was stylized as a fraction on early pressings of the record?

9 What do the following songs have in common: 'At Seventeen', '19th Nervous Breakdown', '59th Street Bridge Song', 'Highway 61 Revisited'?

10 In her song 'Pi', Kate Bush attempts to sing pi to 150 decimal places but gives up after how many numbers?

ANSWERS

1 Sixteen.

Lyricist Keith Reid specified that there would be sixteen Vestal Virgins leaving for the coast, which was ten more than had been required to tend the eternal flame in the temple of Vesta in ancient Rome.

2 To ten.

The song, which was originally composed by Australian songwriter Sally Seltmann before becoming a hit for Feist, goes all the way to double figures in its final verse.

3 'One-two-three-four-five-six'.

This is what Richman shouts at the beginning of both recordings of 'Roadrunner', by the Modern Lovers and in his own right.

4 Three.

There are three members of De La Soul, of course; but the inspiration for their song 'The Magic Number' comes from a song called 'Three Is A Magic Number', which was featured in a popular programme on American children's TV in the 1970s called *Schoolhouse Rock!*

5 Trigonometry and algebra.

In the song, which Cooke co-authored with Lou Adler and Herb Alpert, he sings 'don't know much trigonometry, don't know much about algebra'. He also adds that he doesn't know what a slide rule is for. Since their functions have been usurped by the pocket calculator this is less of a problem now than it might have been when the song was composed. The slide rule was such an important piece of equipment in the 1960s that Buzz Aldrin took one with him to the moon.

6 Van der Graaf Generator.

A Grounding In Numbers featured a track called 'Mathematics' which refers to Euler's Identity (or, as we all know it, $e^{i\pi} + 1 = 0$).

7 No.

The name 10cc occurred to their then-producer Jonathan King in a dream. It was only in subsequent years that the members of the band took to telling interviewers that the name derived from the cubic capacity of the average male ejaculation (which is 9cc, and therefore the members of the band, being Mancunians, would hope to be able to provide the full 10). A classic case of the myth being halfway around the world before the truth has got its pants on.

8 'Love Minus Zero/No Limit'.

Dylan has said that the proper title of this song from his album *Bringing It All Back Home* should be a fraction with 'Love Minus Zero' on the top and 'No Limit' on the bottom and that it appeared in this form on early pressings of the record. Since that time the two parts of the title have been separated only by an oblique.

9 They all contain prime numbers.

In other words, the number in each song title can only be divided by one and itself.

10 Seventy-eight.

When Kate Bush decided to write a song about the mathematical constant expressed as π she wanted to see how it would feel to sing numbers as though they had emotional value and it was her plan to sing pi to 150 decimal places. In the event she got as far as singing the first seventy-eight (employing some artistic licence on the fifty-fourth digit), then missed out the next twenty-two before resuming.

'School was a very cruel environment, and I was a loner. But I learned to get hurt, and I learned to cope with it.'

Kate Bush

SCHOOL TRIP:
NEW YORK

All five Ramones greet visitors to the Apple.

QUESTIONS

In the spoken section of his 'Living For The City', Stevie Wonder plays the rube emerging from the bus station, looking up at the buildings and saying, 'New York! Just like I pictured it.' It's a city that's had the same effect on almost every songwriter and musician who landed in it, smelled its hot dogs, looked at the steam rising from its pavements, stepped smartly to avoid a yellow cab and thought, 'If I can make it here I can make it anywhere.'

1 Which intersection does Lou Reed recommend for the keen seeker of drugs in the Velvet Underground song 'I'm Waiting For The Man'?

2 In the lyrics of the Pogues and Kirsty MacColl song 'Fairytale Of New York', 'Galway Bay' is being sung by the members of which city choir?

3 The New York City heatwave of 1966, during which temperatures were over ninety degrees for thirty-four days, inspired a fifteen-year-old to compose a song which his elder brother's band made into a worldwide hit. What's the name of the song?

4 The 2004 Beastie Boys single 'An Open Letter To NYC' came from an album titled *To The 5 Boroughs*. Can you name the five boroughs of New York?

5 The cover of the 1980 Supertramp album *Breakfast In America* features a waitress in place of the Statue of Liberty. What is she holding instead of the torch?

6 Which artist's video for 'New York, New York' featured the twin towers of the World Trade Center and was filmed just four days before 9/11?

7 When the Beatles played New York's Shea Stadium in 1965, breaking all records for attendance at a pop show, they only played a short set. How many songs?

8 When the Who performed *Tommy* at New York's Metropolitan Opera House in 1970, pinball machines were actually illegal in the city. True or false?

9 Of all the many images taken at New York's Studio 54, few are more memorable than the one taken of Bianca Jagger in the club on 2 May 1977. What made it so remarkable?

10 A famous Leonard Cohen song refers to his experience of being fellated by Janis Joplin in one of New York's most famous hotels. Can you name it?

ANSWERS

1 Lexington/125.

The protagonist of the song, which first appeared on the album *The Velvet Underground And Nico* in 1967, waits for his drug dealer at the intersection of the uptown street Lexington Avenue and the crosstown street 125th Street in Harlem.

2 The boys of the NYPD choir.

This is obviously the choir of the New York Police Department, an organization that traditionally recruited from the city's many people of Irish descent. Interestingly, there is no such choir.

3 'Summer In The City'.

It was originally written by teenager Mark Sebastian as he looked out of the window of the family's home on posh Washington Square and dreamed of being allowed to join the bohemian girls who danced there. It was taken up by his elder brother John's group the Lovin' Spoonful and made into a global smash that's still played on the radio today.

4 Manhattan, Brooklyn, Queens, the Bronx and Staten Island.

5 A glass of orange juice on a plate.

The cover features actress Kate Murtagh dressed as the waitress.

6 Ryan Adams.

He shot the video for 'New York, New York' in Brooklyn with the Manhattan skyline, inevitably including the World Trade Center, in the background. When the video was eventually broadcast there was a message at the end paying tribute to those who had lost their lives.

7 Twelve.

The Beatles set lasted half an hour, and four of the twelve were songs they didn't write.

8 True.

Pinball remained against the law in many major cities across America until the middle of the decade. Their reasoning was that pinball was a game of chance not skill and therefore needed to be regulated like other forms of gambling.

9 She is on a white horse.

She did not ride the animal into the club, she claims – it was already there.

10 The Chelsea Hotel.

The song is 'Chelsea Hotel No. 2' from 1974. The lyrics don't actually mention Janis but they do describe somebody 'giving me head on the unmade bed' and in subsequent interviews he confessed that it was about her. He also adds, 'You told me again you preferred handsome men, but for me you would make an exception.' When Cohen bumped into her in the Chelsea Hotel she was actually looking for Kris Kristofferson. 'I'm Kris Kristofferson,' said Cohen.

'*She would not have minded. My mother would have minded.*'

Leonard Cohen on Janis Joplin

Neil Tennant interviews Paul Weller under the stern gaze of Pavarotti.

MEDIA STUDIES

QUESTIONS

Seen in certain lights, popular music itself is almost a part of the media. Its relationship with the radio is symbiotic, its historical dependence on television is very nearly pathetic, and music's relationship with the press is like that of two shameless old tarts who often find themselves sharing a cell at the end of an evening of over-indulgence at an awards night. This section is dedicated to this sometimes tawdry traffic.

1 The following acts all had hit singles that share their names with which famous magazines?

    a) the Style Council
    b) Madonna
    c) Lionel Richie
    d) Culture Club

2 What media profession do the Boomtown Rats, the Pet Shop Boys and Cockney Rebel have in common?

3 What was the 1970 number one hit that was only cleared for radio play on the BBC after the singer had made a special journey across the Atlantic to overdub two syllables on a controversial brand name?

4 During the Live Aid broadcast in 1985, Phil Collins flew across the Atlantic on Concorde so that he could say he played with two acts on different sides of the Atlantic on the same day. Who were the two acts?

5 What were the names of the artists whose tunes were used to introduce the following TV music shows?

> **a)** *Ready Steady Go!*
> **b)** *The Old Grey Whistle Test*
> **c)** *Top of the Pops*
> **d)** *The Word*
> **e)** *The Tube*

6 Which band was engaged to improvise live in the BBC studios during the Corporation's coverage of the moon landings in 1969?

7 What special variety of television did the Beatles, the Jackson Five, the Monkees, New Kids on the Block and MC Hammer have in common?

8 The island of Jura in the Inner Hebrides was in 1994 the site of one of the most talked-about stunts in the history of pop. What was it, and who did it involve?

9 Who accidentally-on-purpose exposed a nipple during the half-time show at the 2004 Super Bowl, and how was it explained away the following day?

10 *Razzmatazz*, *Gastank*, *Beat in the Border*, *Campus Rock*, *Check It Out*, *Planet Pop* and *Rockin' the Box* – all genuine, long-forgotten music programmes on British TV. Except one – but which one?

ANSWERS

1
  a) the Style Council did 'Paris Match'
  b) Madonna had a hit with 'Vogue'
  c) Lionel Richie recorded 'Hello'
  d) 'Time' was one of Culture Club's hits

2 Journalism.

All three have lead singers who worked as journalists before turning to music. Bob Geldof worked as a music journalist in Canada, Neil Tennant was on the staff at music magazine *Smash Hits*, and Steve Harley worked as a reporter on various newspapers in east London.

3 'Lola'.

In 1970 the BBC would not play the Kinks' single as long as the lyrics referred to Coca-Cola. Since the Kinks were on tour in the USA at the time and the master tapes were in London, Ray Davies had to fly back to change Coca-Cola to the more generic 'cherry cola'. The first session did not go according to plan so Davies had to make another return transatlantic flight before it was done to his satisfaction.

4 Sting (Wembley) and Jimmy Page, Robert Plant and John Paul Jones of Led Zeppelin (Philadelphia).

In both venues Collins also performed in his own right.

5 a) Manfred Mann ('5-4-3-2-1')
b) Area Code 615 ('Stone Fox Chase')
c) CCS ('Whole Lotta Love'). CCS's was the instrumental version of Led Zeppelin's hit, and was the show's most-used theme music. Thin Lizzy were responsible for the other long-running *Top of the Pops* theme 'Yellow Pearl'.
d) 808 State ('Olympic')
e) Jeff Beck ('Star Cycle')

6 Pink Floyd.

They improvised a tune which they called 'Moonhead'. 'It was fantastic to be thinking that we were in there making up a piece of music, while the astronauts were standing on the moon,' recalled David Gilmour forty years later.

7 Children's TV.

Each of the five acts had a cartoon series based on their adventures.

8 On 23 August 1994, Bill Drummond and Jimmy Cauty of the K Foundation burned cash amounting to a million pounds – money from the huge success of records they had made under the name the KLF – in a disused boathouse on the island.

9 Janet Jackson.

In the course of their performance together at Super Bowl XXXVIII, Justin Timberlake exposed one of Janet Jackson's nipples. This was later blamed on 'a wardrobe malfunction'.

10 *Razzmatazz*, which introduced Lisa Stansfield to the public, was a children's music programme that ran between 1981 and 1987. Just six episodes of *Gastank*, a 'musos jamming' format co-hosted by Rick Wakeman, were broadcast in 1983. *Beat in the Border* was a Border Television production from 1962. *Campus Rock* was the BBC Northern Ireland version of *Rock Goes to College*. *Check It Out* was a youth show with a music slant which came from the north-east between 1979 and 1982. *Planet Pop* aired on Channel 4 between 1998 and 2000. *Rockin' the Box* is the odd one out because I made it up.

PERSONAL, SOCIAL AND HEALTH EDUCATION

Sly Stone and Kathy Silva had a quiet wedding.

QUESTIONS

This is an umbrella beneath which you can find all the subjects that people say really ought to be taught at school but aren't. Here you might find matters spiritual, social and moral as well as sexual. In this round we lean heavily on the rich and often hilarious history of rock stars and marriage.

1 How many times were the members of the Beatles married in total?

2 What was particularly noteworthy about Sly Stone's marriage to Kathy Silva in 1974?

3 Which two of these celebrated couples never actually got married?

    a) Mick Jagger and Jerry Hall
    b) Lisa Marie Presley and Michael Jackson
    c) Paul Simon and Carrie Fisher
    d) Chrissie Hynde and Jim Kerr
    e) Rod Stewart and Britt Ekland

4 What marriage links the J. Geils Band of 'Centerfold' fame and the movie *Chinatown*?

5 Which was the shortest-lived of these three marriages?

    a) Pamela Anderson and Kid Rock in 2006
    b) Britney Spears and Jason Alexander in 2004
    c) Cher and Gregg Allman in 1975

6 The most commercially successful song in praise of illegal drugs was number one in Britain in 1982. What was it?

7 Which three famous musicians became known in later life by these names?

    a) Jikan
    b) Yusuf Islam
    c) Sananda Maitreya

8 What religious tradition were Patti Smith, Michael Jackson and Geri Halliwell all raised in?

9 What do the Coasters' 'Poison Ivy', Eminem's 'Drips' and 'The Jack' by AC/DC all have in common?

10 What was the inspiration behind Paul Simon's song 'Mother And Child Reunion'?

ANSWERS

1 Nine times.

John married Cynthia in 1962 when she was expecting their son Julian, then Yoko Ono in 1969, shortly after Paul McCartney had married for the first time, to Linda Eastman. After Linda died in 1998 Paul married Heather Mills, in 2002. He divorced her in 2008, marrying Nancy Shevell in 2011. George Harrison married Pattie Boyd in 1966 and divorced her eleven years later. He subsequently married Olivia Arias, in 1978. Ringo Starr married Maureen Cox in 1965 and divorced her in 1975. He has been married to Barbara Bach since 1981.

2 The wedding of Sly Stone and model-actress Kathy Silva took place in front of thirty thousand guests on stage at Madison Square Garden during a sold-out performance on 5 June 1974. They separated two years later after his dog mauled the couple's child.

3 a) Mick Jagger and Jerry Hall, and e) Rod Stewart and Britt Ekland.

Jerry Hall thought she was married to Mick Jagger, having gone through some species of ceremony in Bali in 1990. It was only ten years later, when the couple had broken up, that the High Court in London decided that the marriage was invalid.

Between 1975 and 1977 Rod Stewart and Britt Ekland were Britain's foremost celebrity couple, but they never married. One of the strangest aspects of the strange life of Michael Jackson was his two-year marriage to Elvis Presley's daughter Lisa Marie in 1994. He was married to her when he impregnated Debbie Rowe, who at the time was working as the assistant to his dermatologist. The two married following his divorce from Presley. Paul Simon was married to Carrie Fisher between 1983 and 1984. Jim Kerr was married to Chrissie Hynde between 1984 and 1990.

4 The J. Geils Band lead singer Peter Wolf married actress Faye Dunaway, star of *Chinatown*, in August 1974 in Beverly Hills. They split up in 1978.

5 b) Britney Spears and Jason Alexander.

Pamela Anderson and Kid Rock got married in July 2006 and Pamela filed for divorce in November of the same year. Cher and Gregg Allman separated just a week after their marriage but then got back together when she turned out to be pregnant, divorcing two years later. However, the all-comers record for short-lived marital union was Britney Spears' Las Vegas marriage to her old friend Jason Alexander which was annulled after just fifty-five hours, which is shorter than a Test match.

6 'Pass The Dutchie' by Musical Youth.

The song by the teenage group from Birmingham was an adaptation of 'Pass The Kouchie' by the

Mighty Diamonds, 'kouchie' being slang for a pot in which marijuana is kept. 'Pass The Dutchie' was the fastest-selling single of 1982 in the UK, shifting a hundred thousand copies in a single day.

7

a) Leonard Cohen was given the name Jikan (which variously translates as 'Silent One' or 'Silence') when he was ordained as a Zen monk and retired to live on Mount Baldy in California in 1994

b) Cat Stevens took the name Yusuf Islam after he embraced Islam

c) Terence Trent D'Arby changed his name to Sananda Maitreya in 1995

8

The parents of all three were practising Jehovah's Witnesses.

Smith claims this is what gave her a strong grounding in the Bible, Halliwell remembers life being difficult when she was young because her mother didn't agree with birthdays or Christmas, while even at the height of his fame Michael Jackson disguised himself before knocking on doors to proclaim his faith. He ceased being involved with the Witnesses in 1987.

9

They're all about sexually transmitted diseases.

10

The title has little to do with human relationships: it came from a chicken and egg dish called a 'Mother and child reunion' that Paul Simon saw on the menu of a Chinese restaurant.

PHYSICS

Magma: favourite group of interesting snooker champion.

QUESTIONS

'The stars are matter. We're matter. But it doesn't matter.' This was what Captain Beefheart had to say on the subject of physics, which is of course the study of matter, space, time and the other forces governing the universe. Here are ten questions dealing with those times when pop has come into contact with these elemental issues.

1 Talking about a song he wrote which had been inspired by quantum physics, in 2002 Moby explained that 'on a basic quantum level, all the matter in the universe is essentially made up of . . .' what?

2 Which world-famous singer, who invested in new technology all his life, pioneered the use of tape recording in the years after the Second World War?

3 What's the 1964 Beatles hit that begins with the deliberate sound of feedback?

4 The middle name of Jimi Hendrix was the same as that of the British company that built a worldwide reputation for the loudest amplifiers. What is the name of the company?

5 The lyrics of which Queen hit record referred to the physicist whose theories led to his being tried by the Inquisition and forced to recant?

6 When Thomas Edison unveiled his first phonograph, which dazzled the world by proving it was possible to record and play back human speech, he did a demonstration with which nursery rhyme?

7 Is there a dark side of the moon?

8 What is the name of the French progressive rock band, formed in 1969, who sang their songs in their own invented language?

9 Which of these songs was inspired by a real thing: 'TVC 15' by David Bowie, 'CTA-102' by the Byrds, '2112' by Rush?

10 The name of the band Earth, Wind and Fire contains two of the classical elements. Which one shouldn't be there and which other two should be?

ANSWERS

1 Stardust.

He said this because his new tune was called 'We Are All Made Of Stars', an assertion physicists essentially agree with. As planetary scientist Dr Ashley King explains, 'Nearly all the elements in the human body were made in a star and many have come through several supernovas.'

2 Bing Crosby.

He was a very shrewd businessman. He invested in the company that pioneered frozen orange juice, in the Pittsburgh Pirates baseball team, and in the fledgling tape company Ampex. American soldiers had come back from the war in Europe with technology developed by the Nazis which had enabled Hitler's speeches to be heard around the country. Crosby, who at the time had to do his weekly radio show live, invested because he was attracted by the idea of pre-recording and editing the show to a standard that had been previously impossible.

3 'I Feel Fine'.

The first deliberate use of feedback, which is the sound created when the pickup of the guitar is placed too near the amplifier, thereby picking up the sound coming from the amplifier and amplifying it further, came at the start of this Beatles hit.

4 Marshall.

In the sixties and seventies Marshall, started by former dance band drummer Jim Marshall from west London, built amplifiers for all the loudest British bands, from the Who on down.

5 'Bohemian Rhapsody'.

The song references the sixteenth-/seventeenth-century Italian astronomer, physicist and polymath Galileo Galilei. His theory that the Earth and planets revolved around the sun brought him into conflict with the teachings of the Church at the time: they preferred to believe that the rest of the universe revolved around the Earth and its most prominent inhabitant, man. Galileo escaped being sent to prison but spent the rest of his life under house arrest.

6 'Mary Had A Little Lamb'.

The earliest known recording of an American voice (Edison's) was committed to tin foil in 1877. Nearly a century later, in 1972, Wings had a top ten hit in the UK with Paul McCartney's version of the classic rhyme.

7 No.

There is one hemisphere of the moon that always faces away from Earth but, like the side that faces us, it experiences two weeks of sunlight followed by two weeks of night. When we talk about the dark side of the moon we mean the side that remains unseen to us rather than one that lacks light.

8 Magma.

Magma is the molten material found at the centre of the Earth. The snooker player Steve Davis, who is one of the band's most devoted fans, recalled, 'I saw them when I was seventeen. It was the most musically life-changing experience of my life.' He remains a fan. Magma named their invented language Kobaïan.

9 'CTA-102'.

'TVC 15', which is on Bowie's 1976 album *Station To Station*, was a fantasy inspired by Iggy Pop's drug-addled hallucination that the TV could swallow people. '2112' in the Rush song has no particular significance. The lyrics were allegedly based on the novella *Anthem* by Ayn Rand. 'CTA-102', however, was the name of a quasar discovered in the early 1960s which captured the imagination of the aeronautically disposed Jim McGuinn of the Byrds who took it as a sign of extraterrestrial intelligence.

10

Wind shouldn't be; air and water should.

Earth, air, water and fire are the four classical elements. When the band was formed in the late 1960s, leader Maurice White substituted wind for air in honour of the group's horn section.

President and rock star in the days when the latter was the crazy one.

QUESTIONS

Ever since Bob Dylan became well known with songs that referred to the political sphere it has seemed that we are never more than half an hour away from an earnest discussion about what might have happened to the supposedly close relationship between politics and pop. Here are ten questions deriving from that strange affair.

1 What well-known song from 1974 was the South's response to Neil Young's characterization of the southern United States as the home of cross burning and bullwhip cracking in his song 'Southern Man'?

2 When he was at university, Tony Blair was in a band called Ugly Rumours. What role did he play in the band?

3 What was the hit-making jazz rock band of the late sixties who got their name from a speech by Winston Churchill?

4 Which hip hop musician announced his intention of running for the presidency of Haiti?

5 Sonny Bono of sixties hitmakers Sonny & Cher was elected to the US Congress in 1994. How did he die in 1998?

6 When Elvis Presley turned up unannounced at the White House in 1970 what did he want from Richard Nixon?

7 What do Prince's 'Purple Rain', Pharrell Williams' 'Happy', the Rolling Stones' 'Start Me Up' and Neil Young's 'Rockin' In The Free World' have to do with Donald Trump?

8 Bob Marley was famously photographed linking hands with bitter political rivals Michael Manley and Edward Seaga at the One Love Peace Concert in Jamaica in 1978. When Bono repeated the moment at a concert in Belfast before the referendum on the Good Friday Agreement in 1998, whose hands did he hold aloft?

9 Which musician announced he would be running for president in 2020 at the 2015 MTV Awards?

10 Which two of these four British singers have come out in favour of Brexit: Morrissey, Mick Jagger, Billy Bragg, Roger Daltrey?

ANSWERS

1 'Sweet Home Alabama' by Lynyrd Skynyrd.

This song was the biggest hit of the Southern rock boomlet of the mid-seventies, and contains the line 'I hope Neil Young will remember, a southern man don't need him around'.

2 Singer.

Ugly Rumours were formed at Oxford University in the early seventies. Blair got the job because none of the rest of the band fancied singing, and he arrived at the audition having carefully written out the lyrics to songs such as the Rolling Stones' 'Live With Me'. Fellow member Mark Ellen remembers him taking to the stage at the Corpus Christi Alternative Ball wearing low-slung flares, baring his midriff and wagging his finger at the audience Mick Jagger-style.

3 Blood, Sweat & Tears.

When they put the house lights on at the end of an all-night session at a New York club, Al Kooper noticed there was blood on the organ. At that moment he decided that the perfect name for his new group was Blood, Sweat & Tears, which is almost a lift from Churchill's speech, the only difference being that Churchill promised 'toil' as well.

4 Wyclef Jean.

Jean was born in Haiti in 1969 but made his name in the United States with the Fugees. Following the 2010 Haiti earthquake he was prominent in raising funds for disaster relief and announced he would be running for president. Unfortunately he was ineligible because he hadn't been living in the country for the five-year period required.

5 Sonny Bono hit a tree while skiing near Lake Tahoe in California.

6 A badge.

When Elvis decided on his own initiative to fly to Washington and see President Nixon, his number one priority was to get the credentials of a federal agent in order to assist in the war on illegal drugs. He had already been given deputy's badges by many of the cities he had visited and wanted something similar to prove that he was working on behalf of the government. This request was at first refused, but since he mentioned it again when he met the President the powers-that-be eventually relented and came up with a badge.

7 These are just some of the records that have been used to rev up the crowds at Trump rallies. In each case 'cease and desist' letters have been issued on behalf of the artist, or they have voiced an objection. These objections have had no effect because under US law any music can be played in a public building without permission of the creator.

8 David Trimble's (leader of the Ulster Unionists) and John Hume's (leader of the Social Democratic and Labour Party, the SDLP).

9 Kanye West.

He made the pledge before Trump's election. Since then he has appeared in more than one awkward media engagement with the President and claimed that he is disavowing his interest in politics and 'focusing on being creative'.

10 Morrissey and Roger Daltrey.

Both have expressed their support for Brexit. Jagger and Bragg have released records that make clear their disagreement with it.

RELIGION

Alice Cooper before being born again.

QUESTIONS

The three founding fathers of rock & roll, Elvis Presley, Little Richard and Jerry Lee Lewis, all pinched their acts from the flamboyant preachers of their childhood and regarded their music as a permanent battle between the aspirations of the spirit and the desires of the flesh. Hence these ten questions about the traffic between the two.

1 Which legendary heavy rocker and storied debaucher began his career as a member of a group called the Rockin' Vickers?

2 Who walked out on a successful band in the middle of a 1971 tour, went to live with a religious sect and demanded henceforth to be addressed as Jonathan?

3 Which major superstar no longer plays concerts on Friday nights out of respect for the Sabbath, despite not actually being Jewish?

4 Which country performer and humorist, known for such songs as 'They Ain't Makin' Jews Like Jesus Anymore' and 'Get Your Biscuits In The Oven And Your Buns In The Bed', claimed he was the first Jew to play the Grand Ole Opry?

5 Which veteran rock star, who was raised by a father who was a pastor and who credits his Christian faith with rescuing him from alcoholism, played King Herod in a star-studded 2018 revival of *Jesus Christ Superstar*?

6 Which faith organization do Beck, Edgar Winter and Chick Corea all subscribe to?

7 Who said 'A few years ago I thought I truly was possessed by the devil. I remember sitting through *The Exorcist* a dozen times, saying to myself, "Yeah, I can relate to that"'?

8 Which one of these three hard rock bands has a name that actually derives from the Bible: Black Sabbath, Avenged Sevenfold, Judas Priest?

9 What religious beliefs did the most fabled figure in reggae, Marcus Garvey, espouse?

10 What is heaven, according to songs by the following artists?
a) Talking Heads
b) Belinda Carlisle
c) Traffic

ANSWERS

1 Lemmy.

Formed initially in Blackpool as the Rev. Black and the Rocking Vicars, the band moderated their name to the Rockin' Vickers in the latter part of the 1960s, by which time their guitarist was Ian Kilmister, who was to become more famous as Lemmy, the leader of Motörhead.

2 Jeremy Spencer.

Spencer was one of the stars of Fleetwood Mac when a combination of road fatigue and mescaline nudged him into a sudden religious conversion. In 1971 he walked out on the afternoon of a gig in Los Angeles without telling the rest of the band. They found him days later living with a group called the Children of God under the name Jonathan. He is still with the group, who now prefer to be known as the Family International.

3 Madonna.

Since embracing the teaching of Kabbalah, Madonna no longer performs on Friday evenings out of respect for the Jewish foundation of the faith. Madonna Louise Ciccone was raised in the Catholic Church and was never slow to exploit the imagery of the Church in such videos as 'Like A Prayer'.

4 Richard 'Kinky' Friedman.

A proud Texan, friend of presidents, member of Bob Dylan's Rolling Thunder Revue, singer, crime novelist, candidate for office and prominent cigar aficionado, Friedman has maintained a profile on the fringes of entertainment for more than fifty years by exploiting the Jewish possibilities of country music. His parody of Merle Haggard's 'Okie From Muskogee' is called, inevitably, 'Asshole From El Paso'.

5 Alice Cooper.

Vincent Furnier was brought up in the Church of Jesus Christ and grew up to become the lead singer and earthly representative of Alice Cooper, in which capacity he outraged Mary Whitehouse and other moral arbiters with his stage presentations. Now in his seventh decade of touring he describes himself as a born-again Christian.

6 The Church of Scientology.

All three are practising members of the organization which has had a lot of success recruiting members of the acting profession.

7 Ozzy Osbourne.

This is what Ozzy said to *Hit Parader* magazine back in 1984. It's hard to know how much credence to give to his association with the dark side but it's difficult to imagine anyone sitting through *The Exorcist* a dozen times.

8 Avenged Sevenfold.

The phrase 'avenged sevenfold' is from Genesis 4:24. Black Sabbath came from a poster advertising a shlock horror film. Judas Priest was inspired by Bob Dylan's song 'The Ballad Of Frankie Lee And Judas Priest'.

9 Although the Jamaican Rastafarians seized on Garvey's predictions that a black king would be crowned in Africa and placed him at the centre of their faith, Garvey himself was raised as a Methodist and became a Catholic.

10
a) Talking Heads regarded heaven as a place where nothing ever happens
b) Belinda Carlisle's hit asserted that it was a place on earth
c) Traffic's song countered that heaven was in your mind

SCIENCE AND TECHNOLOGY

Some records are for export only.

55-33558-002

QUESTIONS

There was a time when the college of musical knowledge might have looked down on the sciences as a body of activity with little or nothing to offer the essential business of reeling and rocking. Since the digitization of every aspect of music we now realize this is no longer a defensible position and so insist all our students have a grasp of the workings of the physical world and the way the sciences have responded to it.

1 In the United States there are gold discs, platinum discs and then, for the highest sales, diamond discs. Strictly speaking this is wrong because diamond is not a metal. The discs really should be named after which metal, the only one more precious than platinum?

2 Which singer left a massively successful act in the early 1970s to be a maths teacher?

3 Lester Polsfuss was one of the most innovative musicians and recording experts in music business history. Under what name is he better known?

4 Which guitarist wrote 'A Survey of Radial Velocities in the Zodiacal Dust Cloud'?

5 Which guitarist has advised the US government on missile technology?

6 What does MP3 stand for?

7 What did Thomas Dolby have to do with the most-played tune on earth?

8 The video of which hit song used a Hollywood star to tell the story of Austrian scientist Wilhelm Reich and his invention of a machine that was supposed to produce rain?

9 There are three major types of rock. What are they?

10 When the two *Voyager* spacecraft were launched in 1977 they carried two records containing a wide range of sounds from our civilization. As well as speech in many different languages, the records contain examples of music including one pop song. What was it?

ANSWERS

1 Rhodium.

The price of rhodium is volatile, but because it can only be mined in certain areas and can only be found in platinum ores it remains the world's most precious metal.

2 Art Garfunkel.

In 1972, Garfunkel got married, moved to Connecticut and began teaching mathematics, the subject he had studied at university, at the Litchfield Preparatory School.

3 Les Paul.

Lester Polsfuss was such an important pioneer of both the electric guitar and multi-track recording that Gibson named a guitar after him.

4 Brian May.

'A Survey of Radial Velocities in the Zodiacal Dust Cloud' is the title of the Queen guitarist's doctoral thesis. It was begun at Imperial College in 1972 and finished over thirty years later.

5 Jeff 'Skunk' Baxter.

The distinctively moustachioed guitarist famous as a member of Steely Dan and the Doobie Brothers became interested in missile technology in the eighties and, encouraged by an engineer neighbour, began to make a serious study of the subject. This led over time to him being called upon to advise and consult for the US government. Consequently he is the only former member of Ultimate Spinach to be granted the security clearance required for access to sensitive information.

6 The audio format MP3 derives its name from the Moving Picture Experts Group who initially developed it. It's formally known as 'MPEG-2 Audio Layer III'.

7 In the early 1990s Dolby moved to California to start a company developing music software. One of the pieces of technology was a synthesizer capable of reproducing polyphonic ringtones which was adopted by Nokia. Twenty years later their ringtone is still estimated to be heard twenty thousand times a second.

8 'Cloudbusting' by Kate Bush.

The song is from her 1985 album *Hounds Of Love*. Movie star Donald Sutherland appears in the video as philosopher and psychoanalyst Wilhelm Reich, Kate plays his son. The clip starts with the two of them hauling Reich's cloudbusting machine to the top of a hill and attempting to point it at clouds in the hope of inducing rain.

9 Igneous, sedimentary and metamorphic.

10 Chuck Berry's 'Johnny B. Goode'.
It's still up there forty-two years later.

'The games industry is already bigger than the music industry, and it's all mainly directed at teenage boys.'

Thomas Dolby

SPORTS SCIENCE

Liverpool's Emlyn Hughes makes prog-rock history.

QUESTIONS

It's amazing to reflect that the Beatles were rarely asked about their sporting loyalties, and when they were, they struggled to appear interested. Nowadays every rock star is expected not just to know about sport but to appear passionate about it. This round explores the relationship between athletic pursuits and the weeds with guitars who always had a note on sports days.

1 Which Pink Floyd record features a recording of the crowd at Anfield singing 'You'll Never Walk Alone'?

2 Roy Harper's 1975 recording 'When An Old Cricketer Leaves The Crease' is widely regarded as one of the most moving musical celebrations of sport. To which two England cricketers was it dedicated?

3 The father of musician and poet Gil Scott-Heron was a professional footballer in the 1950s. Which legendary British club did he play for?

4 The official song for the England team at the 1998 World Cup was credited to England United, which was made up of members of which four English groups?

5 Untold numbers of musicians are also good golfers. Some of them are very good. In 2014 *Golf Digest* published a list of a hundred of them along with their handicaps. Who came top?

6 Which performer began his show at half-time in the 2009 Super Bowl with instructions to the TV audience 'to step back from the guacamole dip ... put the chicken fingers down and turn your television all the way up'?

7 Which football clubs are the following associated with?

a) Roger Waters
b) Robert Plant
c) Rod Stewart
d) Adele
e) Norman Cook

8 Which of these four did not distinguish himself in the boxing ring in his youth?

a) Billy Joel
b) Paul Simon
c) Terence Trent D'Arby
d) Kris Kristofferson

9 Which music superstar made a video in which he went up against a sporting superstar with the same initials?

10 What's the Fleetwood Mac song that became the theme for Formula One coverage in the UK?

ANSWERS

1 'Fearless'.

The track, from Pink Floyd's 1971 album *Meddle*, begins with the recording of the Anfield faithful singing their beloved anthem.

2 Geoff Boycott and John Snow.

Harper's record was the song John Peel wished to have played at his funeral.

3 Glasgow Celtic.

A Jamaican by birth, Gilbert Heron was a professional footballer in both Canada and the United States before playing five games for Celtic in 1951.

4 The Spice Girls, Space, Echo and the Bunnymen and Ocean Colour Scene.

The song, which was called '(How Does It Feel To Be) On Top Of The World', stalled at number nine. Amazingly it got as far as number thirty-eight in Scotland.

5 Vince Gill.

The *Golf Digest* list featured, among many others, Justin Timberlake, Alice Cooper, Huey Lewis, Smokey Robinson and Kenny G, but the country singer Vince Gill was the top musical golfer. Gill has been a scratch player since high school, which means that he can be expected to score par on any golf course. No allowances have to be made for him. He's not quite a top pro but if he was playing with top pros he certainly wouldn't disgrace himself.

6 Bruce Springsteen.

Those are the words with which he began his twelve-minute show with the E Street Band at Super Bowl XLIII.

7
a) Arsenal
b) Wolverhampton Wanderers
c) Glasgow Celtic
d) Tottenham Hotspur
e) Brighton and Hove Albion

8 b) Paul Simon.

Billy Joel and Terence Trent D'Arby both boxed in the Golden Gloves competition as teenagers. Kris Kristofferson was awarded a Blue for boxing at Oxford when he was a Rhodes scholar. Paul Simon never stepped in the ring but he did write a very good song called 'The Boxer'.

9 Michael Jackson.

Jackson's 1992 video for 'Jam' had him play basketball against Michael Jordan and repay the favour by showing him how to dance.

10 'The Chain'.

The track, originally on Fleetwood Mac's *Rumours*, has been used as the theme of Formula One TV coverage since 1978, surviving more than one change in host channel.

The actual Cotton
Club, before fiction
got its hands on it.

THEATRE AND
FILM STUDIES

QUESTIONS

When rock stars dabble in movies they prefer to do it while wearing an outlandish wig or the glad rags of a bygone era. As soon as the film has opened and passed into the tender embrace of obscurity they prefer us to forget all about it. But somehow we can't.

1 Which Californian singer-songwriter played Irving Starck, the cigar-chewing manager of a legendary 1940s nightclub, in a 1984 Francis Ford Coppola film?

2 Which lead singer from west London played a legendary footballer, also from west London, in a 2000 biopic of footballer George Best?

3 Which singer and guitarist was hired to play a mute executioner by the producers of *Game of Thrones* because they had been impressed by his blank expression in a documentary about his band?

4 Which Californian singer-songwriter played a real star of the silver screen in 2004 in Martin Scorsese's film about Howard Hughes?

5 Which poodle-headed rock star played a naval lieutenant in the Second World War film *U-571*?

6 Which androgynous 1980s chart regular kept appearing to whip up the population in a very confusing 1985 film about the American War of Independence?

7 Which American superstar played Pacer Burton, a half-breed youth in the Old West forced to choose between the Kiowa forebears of his mother and the people of his white father?

8 Which American singer played Gloria Tatlock, a missionary nurse trying to find a supply of opium to ease the pain of her patients in pre-revolutionary China, in one of the most notable box office flops of the 1980s?

9 Which guitarist and band leader played a wandering mandolin player who blunders into a family feud in North Carolina in the early days of the American Civil War and ends up marrying one of the film's two stars?

10 Which south London-born star played a German officer returning from the front after the First World War who is forced to find work having sex with attractive women in a brothel?

ANSWERS

1 Tom Waits.

He originated his schtick while entertaining the queues outside the Heritage Coffee House in San Diego, and so it was no surprise that Waits should be given the part of Irving Starck in *The Cotton Club*. 'I spent two and a half months in a tuxedo,' he later recalled. His fondest memory of the project was the time it allowed him to spend with *The Munsters* star Fred Gwynne, who 'had a head bigger than a horse'.

2 Roger Daltrey.

It beggars belief that any film-maker thought it would be possible to convey a fraction of the genius and tragedy of George Best via the medium of acting, but in 2000 somebody actually tried with John Lynch, at the time knocking on middle age, as the eponymous hero of *Best*. Once they had taken on a project this enormous it was but a small step to cast Daltrey, at the time in his mid-fifties, as QPR hero Rodney Marsh.

3 Wilko Johnson.

The producers of *Game of Thrones* could have had their pick of the world's character actors but they decided that only Johnson could play Ser Ilyn Payne, the royal executioner. 'He hasn't been very talkative these last twenty years since the Mad King had his tongue ripped out,' another character explains. Wilko Johnson, by contrast, is literally the most talkative man in rock & roll.

4 Gwen Stefani.

Stefani played the part of thirties blonde bombshell Jean Harlow in *The Aviator*, in which Leonardo DiCaprio played Howard Hughes. This was her first appearance in a movie and to prepare for it she read two Harlow biographies and watched all of the starlet's films. This may not have been the best use of her time because she was only involved in the film for four days and her main surviving contribution is her walk down the red carpet at the 1930 premiere of *Hell's Angels* on Hughes's arm.

5 Jon Bon Jovi.

The part of the unfortunate Lt Pete Emmett, who meets his end when beheaded by flying debris during a naval battle, was taken by the Bon Jovi lead singer. *U-571*, which also starred Matthew McConaughey and Harvey Keitel, caused a minor fuss in Parliament when it was released in 2000 because it pretended that an American vessel had captured the first Enigma machine, when in fact it was a British vessel.

6 Annie Lennox.

In Hugh Hudson's *Revolution*, a film the *New York Times* described as 'so giddily misguided that it's sometimes fun for all the wrong reasons', Al Pacino played a Scottish fur trapper and Donald Sutherland gave his impression of an English sergeant-major. Given that, it was no surprise that the part of the rabble-rousing, flag-waving Liberty Woman should have been taken by Lennox, who was having lots of hits with Eurythmics that year.

7 Elvis Presley.

The script for the 1960 movie *Flaming Star* had been kicking around Hollywood for some years until somebody had the bright idea of casting Presley in the lead role. It came in the period when Elvis had just got out of the army, and suffered commercially because it followed the family-friendly *G.I. Blues*. Critical opinion has since decided that Elvis could actually act and this Don Siegel-directed drama was one of the few films he did that encouraged him.

8 Madonna.

Madonna's love interest in *Shanghai Surprise*, and at the time in real life, was Sean Penn. The producer was George Harrison, who found that even his experience in dealing with delicate egos at the top of fame's greasy pole was not equal to getting the pair of them to cooperate with the press, who were keen to publicize the movie. It landed with a resounding thud, sweeping the boards at that year's Golden Raspberry Awards.

9 Jack White.

In the film adaptation of Charles Frazier's best-seller *Cold Mountain*, Nicole Kidman and Renée Zellweger play the two women forced to hang on to the farm when their menfolk go off to fight. One day, two musicians come wandering by. One of them, a mandolin player who goes by the name of Georgia, catches the eye of Zellweger. He's played by the White Stripes' Jack White, who also wrote and played much of the film's music.

10 David Bowie.

The role of the aristocratic Paul Ambrosius von Przygodski was played by Bowie in the 1978 David Hemmings film *Just a Gigolo* using the exact same nasal monotone he employed in all his parts in films. The people who cast him seemed to exhibit a touching belief that since Bowie was cultured enough to admire actors he would be able to act himself. He couldn't. 'Why are women only interested in sex?' he complains in one of many lines that don't ring entirely true.

PRIZE-GIVING

Odd Couple Sam Fox and Mick Fleetwood host the Brit Awards.

QUESTIONS

Believe it or not there was a time when there were hardly any prizes given out to the members of groups. Nowadays you could go to a different ceremony every night of the week. Whenever a bunch of people who claim to be uncompetitive are gathered together in an openly competitive context the possibilities for comedy – and even farce – are numerous.

1 Past winners of the Outstanding Contribution to Music award at the Brits have included Paul McCartney, U2, Fleetwood Mac, Elton John, Rod Stewart and Van Morrison. Who received the award in 2019?

2 Who made a particularly memorable appearance at the 1985 Brit Awards, making his way to the stage in the hulking slipstream of 6ft 8in bodyguard 'Big Chick' Huntsberry?

3 Which of the following has not been awarded a knighthood by the Queen: Paul McCartney, Mick Jagger, Bob Geldof, Elton John, Rod Stewart, Van Morrison, Phil Collins, Ray Davies?

4 Which artist won the Grammy for Album of the Year in 1974, 1975 and 1977?

5 Michael Jackson swept the board at the 1984 Grammys with his album *Thriller*, taking no fewer than eight awards. Who was his date for the evening, and who did he carry in his arms?

6 Who's the only singer who's had a number one hit record and also won the Oscar in an acting category?

7 When Bob Dylan was awarded the Nobel Prize in Literature in 2016 he was not the first songwriter to be given the prize. Who was the other one?

8 Which band got into hot water for drenching Deputy Prime Minister John Prescott at the Brit Awards in 1998?

9 When Prince appeared at the Brit Awards with the word 'slave' written across his face, how did the British group Blur respond?

10 The Rock & Roll Hall of Fame is known for providing a stage for former members of bands to demonstrate how much they dislike each other. When Dire Straits were invested into the Hall of Fame in 2018 only three members turned up. Which three?

ANSWERS

1 Pink.

The announcement led the *Daily Telegraph* to wonder why the powers-that-be had given this award to somebody 'mediocre and American'.

2 Prince.

He may have been only five foot three but there was not much chance he was going to come to any harm when making his way from his table to the stage at London's Grosvenor House. It didn't appear that he was prepared to take any risks. His huge bodyguard, who in his vest and braces was dressed less for a formal affair in Park Lane than St Patrick's Day in a biker bar, went slowly and gradually before him. Britain sat enthralled as Prince followed to collect his awards for Best International Act and Best Soundtrack. It made his name in the UK.

3 The only one who is not a knight is Phil Collins.

4 Stevie Wonder.

He won in 1974 for *Innervisions*, in 1975 for *Fulfillingness' First Finale* and in 1977 for *Songs In The Key Of Life*. It was a similar story on the other side of the Atlantic. When Paul Simon picked up the Album of the Year award for *Still Crazy After All These Years* in 1976 he thanked Stevie Wonder for not putting out an album that year.

5 Jackson's date for the evening was former child star Brooke Shields. The small person he carried around in his arms was child actor Emmanuel Lewis.

6 Cher.

She has had numerous number one records, and in 1988 she beat Meryl Streep, Holly Hunter, Sally Kirkland and Glenn Close to take the Best Actress Oscar for her role in *Moonstruck*.

7 Rabindranath Tagore.

The Indian poet-songwriter had been awarded the prize in 1913.

8 Chumbawamba.

The water was tipped over Prescott's head by vocalist-guitarist Danbert Nobacon. He didn't have any particular agenda: he said his action was 'a metaphor for the underdog pissing on the steps of Downing Street'. Prescott was seemingly the only authority figure at hand. Nobacon's real name is Nigel.

9 In 1995, when Prince was in dispute with his record company, was referring to himself as 'the artist formerly known as Prince' and was appearing in public with the word 'slave' written on his cheek,

Blur took to the stage to receive their award with their drummer Dave Rowntree identified by the word 'Dave' on his cheek.

10 Bassist John Illsley and keyboard players Guy Fletcher and Alan Clark.

The founder of the band, singer-songwriter Mark Knopfler, had no intention of turning up and his younger brother David cancelled when he realized nobody was picking up his airfare.

'If a representative of the Government has the nerve to turn up at the Brit Awards to be seen as cool and trendy, then he deserves all we can throw at him.'

Chumbawamba 'statement'

Only one of the Beach Boys actually surfed.

HOLIDAY:
LOS ANGELES

QUESTIONS

Today's Los Angeles was a product of the industrial boom of the Second World War period. People flocked there from all over the South in search of its well-paid jobs and congenial climate. In the fifties it became a centre of the record industry as Frank Sinatra and Nat King Cole recorded hit after hit in Capitol's tower in Hollywood. In the sixties and seventies it was the home of the hits of the Beach Boys, the Byrds and Phil Spector. Since then it has become the place every rock star wants to go to, if only to be inspired by its wealth and corruption.

1 Who was the Frankie in Frankie Goes to Hollywood?

2 Cameron Crowe's 1982 movie *Fast Times at Ridgemont High* was based on a public school in which Los Angeles coastal town, a community that also gave its name to the title of a Patti Smith song?

3 What was the collective name given to the Los Angeles session musicians who played on all the great records of Phil Spector, the Beach Boys and Glen Campbell?

4 The two groups most closely associated with the sound of Los Angeles are the Eagles and Fleetwood

Mac. How many of the members of their classic line-ups actually came from the city?

5 What's the only Beatles song named after an address in Hollywood?

6 Which Joni Mitchell album features a picture of the artist naked at the edge of the Pacific Ocean?

7 Which artist wrote most of his early material in Duke's Coffee Shop at the Tropicana Motor Hotel on Santa Monica Boulevard?

8 Which famous protest song was written about a riot at Pandora's Box, a Sunset Strip club, in 1966?

9 Led Zeppelin favoured the Continental Hyatt House when they stayed in Hollywood in the 1970s. John Bonham was said to have ridden a motorbike down the hall. How was the hotel colloquially known at the time?

10 Brian Wilson of the Beach Boys briefly ran a health food store on Melrose Avenue in 1970. What was it called?

ANSWERS

1 Frank Sinatra.

The band name was a fictional headline in a newspaper in an illustration by the Belgian artist Guy Peellaert which pictured a young Sinatra surrounded by swooning bobby-soxers.

2 Redondo Beach.

The film was inspired by the high school at Redondo Beach, just south of Los Angeles, close to where the Beach Boys grew up. 'Redondo Beach' was a song on the first Patti Smith album, *Horses*.

3 The Wrecking Crew.

The group of musicians, which included bassist Carol Kaye, drummer Hal Blaine, pianist Larry Knechtel and guitarist Tommy Tedesco among many others, were referred to as the Wrecking Crew allegedly in recognition of the fact that the older generation of Hollywood pros thought they would wreck the music business.

4 None.

Not a single member of the classic line-ups of these two groups who are most closely associated with Los Angeles came from the city itself. Don Henley was from Texas, Glenn Frey from Detroit, and none of the rest of the group came from LA. Three members of Fleetwood Mac came from the UK, Stevie Nicks was from Arizona, and Lindsey Buckingham came from Palo Alto in northern California.

5 'Blue Jay Way'.

George Harrison composed this song while waiting for Beatles publicist Derek Taylor to find his way to the house he had rented at that address. The song was on the soundtrack of *Magical Mystery Tour*.

6 *For The Roses*.

This 1972 album was initially supposed to feature Joel Bernstein's picture of a naked Joni Mitchell standing on rocks over the Pacific on its cover. Then somebody pointed out the potential indignity of her having a $6.98 sticker over her naked backside and thus it was relegated to the gatefold.

7 Tom Waits.

Tom Waits's friend Chuck E. Weiss was so enamoured of the menu at Duke's Coffee Shop that he moved in. Waits followed him, and it became the perfect background for his emerging persona. He said at the time: 'The place has termites and bad plumbing, you know, and they've just painted the swimming pool black, probably so they don't have to clean it so often. But they take my messages at the desk and gather my mail and I don't have to pay gas or electricity, so it's not so bad.'

8 'For What It's Worth' by Buffalo Springfield.

Stephen Stills wrote the song about the riots that took place on Sunset Boulevard in 1966 when the police tried to crack down on young people assembling to have fun and protest against the Vietnam War.

9 The Continental Riot House.

10 Brian Wilson's short-lived venture went under the name of the Radiant Radish.

Johnny Cash liked to check every record personally.

Q & A WITH
DAVID HEPWORTH

Q This book seems unlike your previous ones.

A True. This one came about following one of those lunches where I try to catch out my editor and my agent with interesting rock-trivia questions. These usually involve the diminutives of the members of Canned Heat, or the reason Ringo Starr's drum parts can't be imitated. After one such lunch, a younger person who had been at the table said, 'Why don't you capture a load of these questions? They'd make a fun book for Christmas.' People in book publishing have a way of describing the writing of books that makes it sound so easy. Well, it wasn't. I can only hope it gives some pleasure, as well as a little bit of frustration.

Q What are you working on next?

A A book about what we call the British Invasion. That is the arrival in America of the Beatles and all the other groups in 1964, and then all the mini-invasions that followed. It strikes me that was an incident without parallel in recent history – when one small nation that had previously been beneath the notice of a big nation suddenly engineered a kind of reverse takeover. As ever, this is a story about music – but it's a story about lots of other things as well. I wanted to write something about what it did to America, and also what it did to Britain. I was in my teens when it began to happen, and I remember it as a great adventure that did a lot for the national self-esteem at a time when it was at a very low ebb. Suddenly all these shrugging, apologetic boys and girls from semi-detached houses in the London suburbs with bad teeth were the coolest people on earth. And without meaning to, they taught their American contemporaries something about their own music. Then the Americans started to add their own learning and the ideas went back and forth. The transatlantic traffic in music and ideas and attitudes and looks has gone on ever since, and it's fascinating to look at how it all worked. We think we're similar because we sing in the same language. We're not similar at all.

Q How long does it take to write your books?

A The actual writing doesn't take all that long. What does take a long time is the business of thinking about the subject matter. My previous three books, *1971: Never a Dull Moment, Uncommon People: The Rise and Fall of the Rock Stars* and *A Fabulous Creation: How the LP Saved Our Lives*, all benefited from dealing with a defined time period. Once you've decided on that, you have to find a workable way to deliver on the promise in the title. I do lots of false starts until I find something that works for me. If it doesn't sound too pretentious, I want to write books that combine a good feeling for what happened in pop music with a solid sense of historical background and then throw in a few ideas to give people something to think about. Whenever I talk to readers who lived through the period I'm writing about, they always mention the things they've been reminded of that they might not have thought about for ages. I find that side of it very gratifying.

Q Was 1971 really the best year in rock music?

A Whenever I talk about this in public, somebody always says, 'Don't you think you should have written about 1973 or 1976 or 1982?' or whatever their favourite year is. I always say, 'If you think that, write your own book, by all means, but please read mine first.' There's no point in trying to dissociate myself from 1971, but the argument of *Never A Dull Moment* is that 1971 was the annus mirabilis of the rock album. That's the key point. You could write a similar book about 1965 being the annus mirabilis of the 7-inch 45 rpm single. Because it was. If you don't believe me, go and look at the singles that came out that year. The 45 was still a relatively young medium at the time, and people were finding out every week what they could do with it. It's the same with 1971 and the album. Pop music is always a question of the coming together of music and technology. It moves on all the time. The reason the pop music of today sounds different from the pop music of, say, the 80s is that it's made using different tools and in a profoundly different way. It'll be different again in another ten years. What's interesting to me is to recognize the differences. I'm not seeking to say one's any better than another.

Q Is 'You Never Can Tell' by Chuck Berry really the best record ever made?

A You can certainly make that argument – and I have done. I tend to choose it for three reasons. The first is that I've always loved it. The second is that I've got a giant print of the original single cover as painted by Morgan Howell above my desk, so it's always front of mind. The third is that I think it perfectly exemplifies the difference between a great song and a great record. 'You Never Can Tell' is a very good song with brilliant lyrics, but its killer charm lies in the way it's performed and captured. It's a better record than most of Chuck Berry's more well-known records. Songs are all very well, but records are a form of magic. John Lennon said that, 'Live performance is all very well, but I'm a record man.' I think I'm the same.

Q Have you seen *Bohemian Rhapsody*, in which your role at Live Aid is taken by an actor?

A No. Although I have seen *Blinded by the Light*, which features my 1984 self. With all this and *Rocketman* and *Yesterday*, I feel it's more important than ever that those of us who were there should set down what we remember. It won't be long before the film industry does to pop history what it did to the Second World War.

Sources

Page 7   'If I'd lived in Roman times, I'd have lived in Rome. Today America is the Roman Empire and now New York is Rome itself.' *John Lennon*
As told by Yoko Ono to Rock Annex curator Jim Henke, article by Amy Plitt, *Time Out New York*, 2009

Page 31   'When things get really bad, just raise your glass and stamp your feet and do a little jig. That's about all you can do.' *Leonard Cohen*
Alex Needham, in the *Guardian*, reporting on an interview between Leonard Cohen and Jarvis Cocker, 2012

Page 65   'The nice thing about "All You Need Is Love" is that it cannot be misinterpreted.' *Brian Epstein*
From *The Beatles Encyclopaedia: Everything Fab Four*

Page 109   'You want the truth? You couldn't afford me.' *Keith Moon*
From the film *The Kids Are Alright*, 1979

Page 117   'A man is a success if he gets up in the morning and gets to bed at night, and in between he does what he wants to do.' *Bob Dylan*
Interview with the *New York Daily News*, spring 1967

Page 133   'Sir, I guess there's just a meanness in this world.'
            Bruce Springsteen
            From his song 'Nebraska'

Page 147   'School was a very cruel environment, and I was a
            loner. But I learned to get hurt, and I learned to
            cope with it.' *Kate Bush*
            From an interview in the *Daily Mirror*, September 2005

Page 155   'She would not have minded. My mother would
            have minded.' *Leonard Cohen on Janis Joplin*
            From an interview in the film *I'm Your Man*, 2006

Page 195   'The games industry is already bigger than the
            music industry, and it's all mainly directed at teenage boys.' *Thomas Dolby*
            Source unknown

Page 217   'If a representative of the Government has the nerve
            to turn up at the Brit Awards to be seen as cool
            and trendy, he deserves all we can throw at him.'
            Chumbawamba
            A 'statement' made by the band, with regards to the Brit Awards 1998

Picture Acknowledgements

Introduction: Debbie Harry in a tour bus en route to Philadelphia: © Martyn Goddard/Getty

Contents: Bill Haley: © Hulton Archive/Getty

American Studies: Bruce Springsteen singing on stage: © Bettmann/Getty

Art: Joni Mitchell and Ronnie Wood: © Brad Elterman Archive/Getty

Biology: Ian Anderson singing: © Hulton Archive/Getty

Business Studies: Heaven 17: © Virginia Turbett/Getty

Classics: Nero and the Gladiators: © Keystone/Getty

Economics: Holly Johnson and Reagan, 1984: © Mirrorpix/Getty

English Language: The Beastie Boys and car: © Dave Hogan/Getty

Fashion and Design: Keith Richards, the Rolling Stones: © Terry O'Neill/Getty

French: Serge Gainsbourg and Jane Birkin: © Alain Nogues/Getty

School Trip – London: The Who: © The Visualeyes Archive/Getty

General Studies: Pink Anderson: © GAB Archive/Getty

Geography: Freddie Mercury and Queen: © Hulton Deutsch/Getty

German: Nena on stage: © Michael Putland/Getty

History: Anni-Frid Lyngstad and Agnetha Fältskog during the Abba concert at the Sydney Showground in 1977: © The AGE/Getty

Home Economics: David Lee Roth: © Fin Costello/Getty

Hospitality Management: Lesley and Mark Carter of Austin, Texas, wait for the start of their third Denver Jimmy Buffett concert: © Denver Post/Getty

Law: Elvis in *Jailhouse Rock*: © Michael Ochs Archives

Literature: Veruca Salt: © Jim Steinfeldt/Getty

Mathematics: Sam Cooke with Cliff White, Los Angeles, 1958: © Michael Ochs Archives/Getty

School Trip – New York: The Ramones: © Chalkie Davies/Getty

Media Studies: Paul Weller, Neil Tennant and Jam: © Virginia Turbett/Getty

Personal, Social and Health Education: Sly Stone and Kathy Silva wedding: © Ron Galella/Getty

Physics: Magma: © Garofalo Jack/Getty

Politics: Elvis and Nixon: © National Archives/Getty

Religion: Alice Cooper with keys: © Terry O'Neill/Getty

Science and Technology: *Voyager* space probe: © Space Frontiers/ Getty

Sports Science: Emlyn Hughes, 1979: © Manchester Daily Express

Theatre and Film Studies: Exterior of Harlem's Cotton Club: © Bettmann/Getty

Prize-giving: Sam Fox and Mick Fleetwood, Brit Awards: © Dave Hogan/Getty

Holiday – Los Angeles: Beach Boys on the beach with a surfboard: © Michael Ochs Archives/Getty

Final Page: Johnny Cash listening to record backstage: © Marvin Koner/Getty

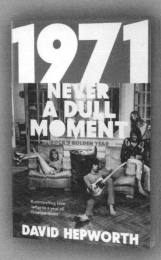

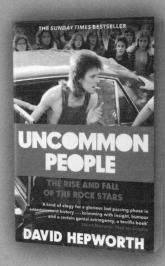

MORE FROM
DAVID HEPWORTH

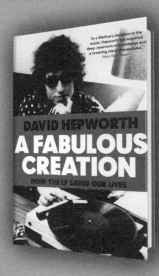

About the Author

David Hepworth is a qualified teacher, but his ambition was to find a job where he could get his hands on free records. This led him into a line of work that has involved writing, broadcasting and speaking about music since the 1970s.

As Editor and Editorial Director, he has been involved in magazines such as *Smash Hits*, *Q*, *Mojo* and *The Word*. As a writer, he has contributed to the *Guardian*, *The Times*, *New Statesman*, *The Face*, *New Musical Express* and *Golf Monthly*, among many others. As one of the presenters of the BBC rock music programme *The Old Grey Whistle Test*, he served as one of the anchors of the corporation's coverage of Live Aid in 1985. He can be seen as himself in the feature film *Blinded by the Light*, and thinly disguised in *Bohemian Rhapsody*.

His previous books, *1971: Never a Dull Moment*, *Uncommon People: The Rise and Fall of the Rock Stars* and *A Fabulous Creation: How the LP Saved Our Lives*, are all *Sunday Times* bestsellers. The first of these is currently being made into a series of films.

He lives in London, dividing his time between writing, speaking at events, broadcasting work, podcasting at www.wordpodcast.co.uk, blogging at www.whatsheonaboutnow.blogspot.co.uk and tweeting @davidhepworth.

David says: 'Pope John Paul II said, "Of all the unimportant things, football is the most important." I feel that way about pop music.'